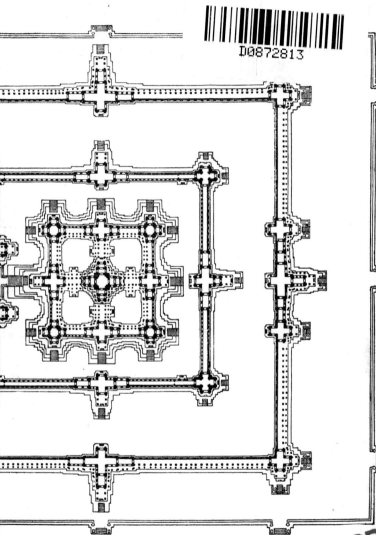

D0872813

ANGKOR
An Introduction

Angkor Wat, the most extensive of all the Khmer monuments, built early in the twelfth century by Suryavarman II, to serve as the temple in which he was worshipped as Vishnu during his life, and where he was entombed, embodied as Vishnu, at his death.

GEORGE CŒDÈS

ANGKOR

AN INTRODUCTION

TRANSLATED AND EDITED BY

EMILY FLOYD GARDINER

PHOTOGRAPHS BY GEORGE BLISS
unless otherwise credited

HONG KONG

OXFORD UNIVERSITY PRESS

LONDON   NEW YORK

Oxford University Press, Ely House, London W.1

GLASGOW NEW YORK TORONTO MELBOURNE WELLINGTON
CAPE TOWN SALISBURY IBADAN, NAIROBI LUSAKA ADDIS ABABA
BOMBAY CALCUTTA MADRAS KARACHI LAHORE DACCA
HONG KONG TOKYO KUALA LUMPUR

96 Tung Lo Wan Road, Causeway Bay

Set by Kenkyusha Tokyo
Reprinted photographically in Hong Kong
by Toppan Printing Co. (HK) Ltd.

Preface to the English Edition

This translation of *Pour Mieux Comprendre Angkor* differs somewhat from the original text published in Hanoi in 1943, and also from the revised second edition published in Paris in 1947 (Bibliothèque de Diffusion of the Musée Guimet, Tome LV).

With my approval some cuts have been made in the text, and some passages have been condensed. The book in its present form omits the history of the changing archaeological theories about Angkor, which are not of special interest to the general reader.

A first-hand acquaintance with the Angkor monuments has been made possible through the work of the Ecole Française d'Extrême-Orient, which, starting in 1907, was responsible for clearing, restoring, and studying the monuments. The work continues today, under the Ecole's technical supervision, with funds supplied by the Royal Government of Cambodia. The present book makes available a brief summary of this accumulated knowledge to English-speaking travellers who are visiting Angkor in ever increasing numbers.

I would particularly like to thank Mrs. Gardiner for the care she has taken with the translation and arrangement of this little book.

Paris, 1961   GEORGE CŒDÈS

Preface to the First Edition

At the request of some of my friends I have gathered into one volume eight lectures which I delivered at the Musée Louis Finot in Hanoi during the last few years. They have not been published before except as brief extracts in the *Cahiers de l'Ecole Française d'Extrême-Orient*. I have amended the original texts to omit repetition, and I have added some bibliographic references.

Each chapter of the book is a separate unit, as was each lecture. Although the chapters are independent of each other, they were all composed with the same purpose, to make available to the public the results of the latest research on Angkor and the Khmer civilization.

Readers will not find here a tourist guide, but rather an introduction to the background of this ancient capital. I have tried to explain the Cambodian monuments in their historical and religious setting, and to dispel the false mystery accumulated through an over-abundant and often mediocre literature. I have attempted to reveal the significance these monuments had for the people who built them. In other words, I have tried to let these great stone structures speak for themselves, because, in the minds of the Khmers, they were never just inert buildings without souls, but monuments with a vital quality that still attracts all who see them.

Hanoi, April 1943   GEORGE CŒDÈS

Contents

List of Illustrations

The Historical and Religious Setting

T HE area covered by the Khmer monuments extends from the Gulf of Siam to Vientiane, and from Saigon to the valley of the Menam, a region corresponding to all present-day Cambodia, the greater part of Indochina, the southern part of Laos and the eastern part of Thailand. Not counting the more distant ruins which were on the furthest outskirts of Cambodia, the domain of Khmer archaeology comprises on the one hand the alluvial plains of the Mekong and the basin of the Grand Lac Tonle Sap, and on the other the plateau of Korat. As will be seen, the attempt to unite these two parts, so different from every point of view, resulted in a political unit which was never stable. The whole history of Cambodia is dominated by the struggle between the peoples of the highlands north of the Dangrek mountains and of the lowlands to the south.

The history of the ancient Khmers, or in other words the Cambodians, is limited to a knowledge of their kings, because our only sources of information are the inscriptions, which relate entirely to the projects of the kings and other high dignitaries.

First there is an early period that we know only through the accounts of Chinese historians. This period extends from the first century through the middle of the sixth century A.D. At that time Cambodia was the centre of a Hinduized kingdom which controlled a large part of the peninsula, and which the Chinese called Funan.[1] This word was a transcription of the Khmer *phnom* meaning mountain. The title of these kings was significant, 'King of the Mountain', and it was after this title that the Chinese named the country.[2]

In the northern part of Funan on the shores of the middle Mekong was the country of the Kambujas. In the middle of the sixth century it was ruled by a prince Bhavavarman of the royal family of Funan, who had married a princess of Kambuja lineage. For some reason not clear to us, he declared himself independent of Funan, and with the help of his brother he made war against the parent state, which thus lost its northern territories and was forced to move its capital to the south. This was the first recorded instance of the continuing antagonism between the north and the south mentioned above. In the seventh century the successors to the two conquering brothers succeeded in annexing more of Funan. One of their kings, Isanavarman, founded a city where the ruins of Sambor Prei Kuk now stand in the province of Kompong Thom. Another king, Jayavarman I, seems to have made his capital for some time at Angkor Borei in Takeo. All this period, from the fall of Funan until the eighth century, is known as the pre-Angkorian period in the history of Cambodia.

The eighth century was disturbed by events we know little about. The country was divided in two, Cambodia of the land to the north, and Cambodia of the sea to the south.[3] Java probably invaded and controlled part of the country.

In the last years of this obscure century a prince who was distantly connected with the former dynasty came back from Java and proclaimed the independence of Cambodia from Java. He instituted a new cult, the cult of the god-king, which was henceforth to be the key feature of Khmer civilization. Abandoning the lower Mekong, he installed himself successively at four different capitals north of the Grand Lac Tonle Sap.[4]

This great king, who was called Jayavarman II, died in 850 near Roluos after forty-eight years of a turbulent reign, in the course of which he had pacified and unified Cambodia, and installed the line of Khmer kings in the region of Angkor for nearly six centuries to come.

His son, Jayavarman III (850–877), and then his nephew, Indravarman (877–889), remained at Roluos. At the death of Indravarman, his son Yasovarman moved the capital several kilometres to the northwest. He gave the name Yasodharapura to this new capital, whose site will be identified later, and in the same neighbourhood he dug the enormous basin known as Baray Oriental. The steles which marked the four corners of this reservoir are still standing.

In 921 King Jayavarman IV abandoned the region of Angkor to build a new capital at Koh Ker, which he decorated with monuments of colossal size. But about twenty years later, in 944, his successor Rajendravarman returned to Angkor where the Khmer kings remained from then on.

Following the reign of Jayavarman V (968–1001), the builder of Banteay Srei and of Takeo, the kingdom for the remainder of the eleventh century was almost entirely in the hands of a dynasty of foreign blood : Suryavarman I (1002–1050), a conquering king from the valley of Menam ; Udayadityavarman II (1050–1066), the builder of the Baphuon ; and Harshavarman III. In 1080, Jayavarman VI, who was not related to any of his predecessors, installed himself, with the help of the Brahman Divakara, as king of a new dynasty which was to last until the fourteenth century. Suryavarman II, who was

one of the greatest kings of Cambodia and the builder of
Angkor Wat, reigned from 1113 to 1150. One can see his
picture at Angkor Wat on the bas-reliefs of the south gallery, where he is represented twice, once seated in the middle of his court and again standing on the back of his elephant. His reign lasted for forty years and was full of daring conquests, which led for a time to the annexation of
part of Champa. There followed a period of fresh troubles
during which the Chams revenged themselves by invading
and destroying Angkor. They were finally driven away by
Jayavarman VII, the last great king of Cambodia, who
was crowned in 1181, and who not only reconstructed the
capital but added an astonishing number of buildings.

After his time his successors began to find themselves
threatened by the Thais, who had recently settled in the
valley of the Menam. This was the beginning of the end,
but the decline of the Khmers was prolonged. It was not
until the middle of the fifteenth century that the court
abandoned Angkor and moved to Phnom Penh, not far
from the ancient capital of Funan and of pre-Angkorian
Cambodia.[2]

We will now see how the Cambodian monuments fitted
into these three different periods, the period of Funan, the
pre-Angkorian period, and the Angkor period.

The only vestiges we are absolutely certain came from
the period of Funan are limited to four Sanskrit inscriptions and a few sculptures. The oldest comes from the
environs of Nha Trang. This is the big stele of Vo Canh,
which for a long time was incorrectly attributed to
Champa. Two others which are Vishnuite come from
Takeo and from Thap-muoi in the Plaine des Joncs. A
fourth, which is Buddhist, was found at Bati.[5] They date
from the third and fifth centuries, and the first half of

the sixth century. Of numerous pre-Angkorian structures situated in central and southern Cambodia in the region which was the centre of Funan, none can be attributed with certainty to the time of Funan. Lacking authentic examples, we can only guess what the architecture of the country was like.

Parmentier tried to attribute several towers situated in southern Cambodia to the artistic tradition of Funan. They are characterized by an absence of false doors and a structure of shallow stories of decreasing size, a form that subsequently disappeared leaving no traces in later architecture.[6]

In sculpture, Vishnuite images from Phnom Da, and a few of the Buddhas of Angkor Borei, give us a good idea of what the sculpture of Funan must have been like and may even date back to the last period of Funan.

Pre-Angkorian Khmer art has been the subject of an exhaustive study by Parmentier.[7] Vestiges of this period are especially abundant in southern Cambodia and in the angle between the Mekong and the Tonle Sap. The most important collection is from Sambor Prei-Kuk, north of Kompong Thom. In architecture the principal monuments are brick towers with a square ground plan, false doors, and mounting stories of decreasing size, each a replica of the one below. The sculptural work was remarkable in its originality. Some fine examples of it can be seen in the museum at Phnom Penh.

The third period from the beginning of the ninth to the end of the twelfth century includes all the monuments of the Angkor group and the great centres at Koh Ker, Prah Khan, Beng Mealea, Banteay Chmar, Prah Vihear, and Phnom Chisor, to mention only the most important and the best known.

Their chronology was long confused because only a few of them were dated with any certainty by inscriptions. The only dates that were definite were those of the temples of the Roluos group, with 879 to 893 engraved on their doors, the group at Koh Ker which was the royal residence for the brief span of twenty-three years from 921 to 944, and Angkor Wat which certainly dates from the early half of the twelfth century. The dating of the other great monuments of the Angkor period has been frequently shifted in the past thirty-five years in accordance with the discovery of new inscriptions, further archaeological evidence, and more advanced research. The full account of the many hypotheses that were advanced and later rejected is too detailed to tell here.[8]

Briefly, Angkor Thom was first thought to correspond to Yasodharapura, built in the ninth century, with the Bayon at its centre, a temple of Siva. A hidden pediment of Lokesvara brought to light at the Bayon in 1924 proved that the monument was at one time Buddhist. Finally, further research indicated that, instead of belonging in the beginning of Angkorian art as had long been thought, the Bayon and the other monuments of the same architectural style, Prah Khan, Ta Prohm, Banteay Kdei, Banteay Chmar, represented the last flowering of Khmer art at the end of the twelfth century.

Banteay Srei, first thought to belong to the fourteenth century, is now known to date from the tenth. Yasodharapura, built by King Yasovarman in the ninth century and first identified with Angkor Thom and the Bayon, is now known to have been centred in Phnom Bakheng.

According to the most recent research the chronology is as follows :

Roluos { Prah Ko		879
Bakong		881
Lolei		893
Phnom Bakheng	*about*	900
The group of Koh Ker	*after*	921
Mebon Oriental		952
Pre Rup		961
Banteay Srei		967
Takeo	*about*	1000
Baphuon	*about*	1060
Angkor Wat	*first half of twelfth century*	
Ta Prohm		1186
Prah Khan		1191
Bayon, gates and walls Angkor Thom		
	end of twelfth century	

The cultural character of the Khmer monuments remains to be considered. The monuments are the product of a Hindu civilization transplanted to Indochina. This does not preclude the originality of Khmer art in relation to its prototypes and its Indian forebears. This originality was marked, and naturally the reason for it was that the artisans who built the temples were Khmers, and were imbued with ancient artistic traditions quite foreign to India. But as soon as one looks behind the external forms for the motivating inspiration, one finds an Indian idea.

One fact is outstanding. Except for some old bridges, every Khmer monument was a religious building. The gods alone had the right to live in houses of stone or brick, the only materials other than bronze that could resist the climate and the passage of time. The sovereigns themselves lived in pavilions of wood. This was a custom that continued in Siam up to the seventeenth century when, under European influence, the kings of Siam began to have their palaces built of brick.

From the time of Funan up to the fourteenth century

the Hindu and Buddhist religions existed side by side in Cambodia. In Funan and in the pre-Angkorian period, Hinduism was mostly represented by the worship of Harihara, who was Siva and Vishnu embodied in a single deity. At the time of Angkor, Siva was the deity most in favour with the royal family. In the twelfth century at the time of Angkor Wat, Vishnu seems to have replaced him.

As for Buddhism, the Lesser Vehicle prevailed at first, and the Sanskrit language was used in the inscriptions. From the ninth to the thirteenth century the inscriptions and images indicate that the Greater Vehicle was in favour. But in the thirteenth century Singhalese Buddhism along with the Pali language spread into Cambodia by way of Siam and soon eliminated the other religions.

[II]

Theories About Angkor

ABOUT one hundred years ago, the naturalist Henri Mouhot wrote an account of his voyages in *Le Tour du Monde*, which for the first time drew the attention of the western world to Angkor. He described it as an architectural creation which perhaps has never had, or ever will have, its equal in the world.

In 1866, six years after the voyage of Mouhot, the mission led by Doudart de Lagrée assembled the first exact data on the Khmer monuments, which were published in 1873 by Francis Garnier in his famous *Voyage d'Exploration en Indochine*. In 1879 the eminent Dutch orientalist, Hendrik Kern, deciphered and translated a Cambodian Sanskrit inscription for the first time, and the first volume of the *Inscriptions Sanskrites du Cambodge* by Auguste Barth appeared in 1885 with the support of the Académie des Inscriptions et Belles Lettres. The very same year that Hendrik Kern started his work on Cambodian epigraphy, Etienne Aymonier, the representative of the French Protectorate, began the series of missions which culminated in the first archaeological inventory of Cambodia, and, even more important, in three hundred and forty rubbings of Sanskrit and Cambodian inscriptions. His book, *Cambodge*, in three volumes, published in 1900, 1901, and 1903, contained all the existent information on Angkor up to the time of the formation of the Ecole Française d'Extrême-Orient in 1898. This latter organization further advanced Cambodian studies, making a complete inventory of the monuments, publishing a considerable number of the inscriptions, clarifying the religious and political history of the Khmer Empire, and establishing the precise chronological order of the great royal monuments and the purposes for which they were intended.[9]

People with a romantic taste for mysterious ruins have always preferred to believe that, in spite of evidence to the contrary, almost nothing was known about the Khmer monuments. For instance in *Pèlerin d'Angkor*, Pierre Loti wrote:

> Here there once were palaces, in which lived those prodigiously luxurious kings, of whom we know nothing, who have passed into oblivion without leaving so much as a name engraved either in stone or in memory.

How much more romantic that sounds than the more accurate introduction to Parmentier's little guide to Angkor Wat:

> The temple of Angkor Wat ... is dedicated to Vishnu, into whose spirit King Suryavarman is supposed to have transmigrated at his death. This event approximately dates the monument, which though uncompleted, must have been mostly constructed in his reign (1113–1145).

The lovers of romanticism have even reproached the French archaeologists for denuding the ruins of the vegetation which obscured them, and for making them both accessible and comprehensible. Unfortunately, we were obliged to choose between clearing the ruins or having them devoured by the forest.

Whether from a love of mystery, or from lack of familiarity with our research, the mistaken opinions I have heard on the origins of the race that built Angkor, on the decline of the Khmer civilization, on the dates of the monuments and the length of time taken for their construction, on the cause of their ruin, and on their character and purpose, are indeed widespread!

In the first place let us take the origin of the Khmers. The most widely held theory is that they came from India. The *Pèlerin d'Angkor* states:

> At some unknown time this city, later completely shrouded by the forest, was one of the wonders of the world. Like the ancient Nile, whose mud gave birth to a great civilization, the Mekong overflowed its banks annually, depositing its riches on the surrounding land, and laid the foundation for the luxurious empire of the Khmers. It was probably at the time of Alexander the Great that a great people migrated from India and settled on the shores of that river after subjugating the cowering native tribes. The conquerors brought with them their Brahman gods and the lovely saga of the Ramayana, and as their prosperity increased on this fertile soil, they built temple after temple, each carved with thousands of figures.

And further on Loti asserts:

> The hardly recognizable ruins of this temple before me represent the primitive conception, simple but savagely powerful, of an isolated people, unlike any others in the world, and with no near neighbours. The Khmer people were a detached branch of the great Aryan race, who settled here by chance, and developed far from their roots, isolated from everything by an immense stretch of forests and swamps.

I have quoted these lines of Pierre Loti not because I attach any scientific authority to *Pèlerin d'Angkor*, but because he expresses in matchless prose one of the erroneous theories that is most generally believed. The civilizing influence of India on Indochina cannot be denied. Its

history certainly exemplifies one of the most remarkable
developments of Hinduism in a foreign country. But to
conclude that the Khmers as a people came in a solid
block from India is too great a step. Judging from their
ethnic and linguistic characteristics, the Khmers, including both the builders of Angkor and the modern Cambodians, belonged to a people who had settled in Indochina in prehistoric times and who spread beyond Cambodia into southern Burma and east to the Annamite
chain.

The dominating aristocracy, particularly in the beginning of the colonization, was most probably of Hindu
blood. But a study of the names of the queens and other
members of the royal family indicates that intermarriage
began early, and that the rigidity of the Hindu caste
system was soon relaxed in this far part of outer India.

At the time of the building of Angkor the royal dynasty
must have been so intermingled with indigenous blood
that there was no question of their being considered
foreign rulers superimposed on the local population. Their
main cultural distinction was their use of Sanskrit writ-
ing. But their portrayal of kings and gods was entirely
typical of the Khmers. Cambodia was the land of Kambu,
the mythical ancestor of the race, and the inhabitants
were the descendants of Kambu, the Kambujas, just as
was their king.

Georges Groslier, with whose ideas I by no means always agree, has given an accurate appraisal of this question. In his book, *A l'ombre d'Angkor*, he too repudiates
the theory of the Indian origin of the Khmers.

> To sum up, classic Cambodia has a clearly primitive and
> aboriginal base. This can be recognized as soon as one
> eliminates first, its economic system and all its connotations,

which are Chinese, and second, its cultural manifestations which are Hindu. Enriched by these two external influences, Khmer art evolved in all its originality and created a hundred elements which are worthy of being ranked with the best in the world.

We conclude then by saying that the Khmers were an indigenous people who were re-invigorated by an admixture of Hindu blood and Brahman culture. But we cannot think of them as coming in a body from India to an uninhabited country, or as having annihilated the indigenous population.

This error has lead to another which is even more false in its ramifications, namely, that the Khmers, having suddenly appeared from abroad on the shores of the Mekong, disappeared just as mysteriously.

As early as 1862 Admiral Bonard wrote in the *Revue Maritime et Coloniale*:

> The history and religion of this vanished people is now exposed to the eyes of the incredulous, so that they can no longer deny that ... the Cambodia we know once nourished and might again nourish a great artistic and energetic race. They can no longer deny it when they see what was created here a few hundred years ago in this land so well-favoured by nature.

The history of the world consists of the rise, the decline, and the final disappearance of powerful empires, but there are very few instances of total submersion or annihilation of a whole people. The Chams, neighbours and ancient rivals of the Khmers, who have been less lucky in that no nation today carries on their name, have still not ceased to exist. Outside the groups of Chams in South Annam, this people who inhabited the coastal region for several centuries still has descendants wearing the typical pantaloons and Annamite turban. If we had a practical

means of estimating the percentage of Chams in the Viet-
namese population of Binh-dinh or of Quang-nam, we
would doubtless be astonished at the figures. And in Cambodia, where we find Khmers who are still called by the
same name and who still speak the same language used by
their ancestors in the inscriptions of the sixth century,
what reason have we to suppose that they are not the
descendants of the great builders? How can we think that
the Khmers disappeared leaving no trace?

I repeat that this civilization is not the only one which
has been known to fall into a total decline after a brilliant
period, due either to unsuccessful wars, or internal strife,
or the inevitable evolution of civilizations.

The sudden decadence of the Khmer people has sometimes been attributed to geographical causes, such as an
earthquake or a catastrophic flood, or a change of climate
accounting for the present uninhabited jungle where once
the country was so thickly populated, and cultivated. But
the fact is well known that a rice-growing country is dependent upon a regulated system of irrigation which in
turn is dependent on a strong and stable central authority. If the control breaks down, the water ceases to work
its benefits, and abundance gives way to misery. As soon
as the production of the flooded rice fields decreases, the
inhabitants resort to burning more land which results in
sterilizing the soil and turning it to laterite, making way
for the harmful effects of deforestation.

The importance in Cambodia of great public enter-
prises was already apparent to Francis Garnier who wrote
in 1869 in the *Revue Maritime et Coloniale*:

> The religious activities which seemed to be the great pre-
> occupation of this civilization were, however, not their only
> interest. In Cambodia one finds the remains of immense

public works, undertaken for the welfare of the people and also in the interest of commerce. These might well have assured a less transitory rule and a greater future to this empire. Magnificent roads, of which we have already spoken, were built into the interior of the country. From place to place immense reservoirs of water, or *srahs*, were constructed, and afforded resting places for the caravans that travelled through. During the six months of the dry season all the small streams dried out, and the two means of transport, the elephant and the buffalo, both required frequent supplies of water. Several excellent bridges are still standing and de Lagrée has discovered vestiges of bridges in the interior of Laos as far north as the fifteenth parallel. These works indicate that there was a dense population and a remarkable degree of prosperity.

In the last years of the thirteenth century, the Chinese Chou Ta Kuen, who stayed some time at Angkor, described the splendours of the kingdom and noted even then some symptoms of decline.[10] 'They say that every man was forced to fight in the war against Siam.' And again, 'In the recent war against Siam the whole country was devastated.' Mass conscription, unsuccessful wars ending in an intentional reduction of the populace by the conqueror, the weakening of central power, and finally a century and a half later, the abandonment of the capital, all these factors serve to account for the contrast between ancient and modern Cambodia which mystifies so many travellers. But all this is no reason to think that the Khmers were a mysterious race now completely vanished. This is a serious error because it deprives the present-day Cambodians of association with their glorious past, and invites their neighbours to infringe on their borders. We will conclude with another passage from *Pèlerin d'Angkor*:

Little Cambodia of today, the conserver of complicated rites, the origin of which has been forgotten, is the last remnant of the vast Khmer Empire which after five hundred years of existence was completely extinguished among the silent trees and the moss. . . . Despite their much reduced kingdom, the Cambodians have remained Khmers, the same people who once astonished Asia with their mysticism and their pomp. Furthermore, they have never given up hope of recovering their ancient capital, shrouded for centuries by the Siamese forests.

The treaty of 1907 fulfilled the hope described in these lines written in 1901.

I will not go into detail about the error made at first in trying to date the ruins of Angkor. The first scholars did not miss by more than a few centuries, even though they did not have access to any of the information which the inscriptions later provided. Mouhot, for example, remained sceptical in spite of the claims of the King of Cambodia 'that he had documents which dated Angkor before the Christian era.' Garnier wrote in 1869:

> One is not in the presence of such antiquity as was first supposed, and it is difficult to date even the oldest of these monuments before the second or third century A.D.

Actually the oldest architectural remains do not antedate the sixth century, and the building of Angkor itself began at the end of the ninth century and continued to the end of the twelfth century.

On the other hand, a similarity noted by quite a few observers and tending to make us think Angkor even more recent than it actually was, must be mentioned. Some of the decorative motifs, especially at Angkor Wat, show a striking resemblance to certain motifs of the Italian Renaissance. Some people think that this resemblance cannot be merely fortuitous, and that consequently we should

---

2. *Apsaras* dancing on the walls of Angkor Wat for the pleasure of the god-king.

3. Angkor Wat, like other Khmer temple-mountains, was a micro-cosm, a replica in stone of Khmer cosmology. The central temple was Mount Meru, the pivot of the world, at whose summit lived the gods.

Its five towers symbolised Meru's five peaks, the enclosing wall represented the mountains at the edge of the world, and the surrounding moat, the ocean beyond.

revise the chronology that places Angkor Wat in the twelfth century, and instead place it after the fourteenth century.

There are a number of circumstances which tend to disprove this theory. Angkor was seen in 1296 by the Chinese Chou Ta Kuen; and in the fifteenth century, Cambodia, in complete decline, would not have been able to erect another similar monument, particularly on an abandoned site, since by then the capital had been moved to Phnom Penh. If there is some connexion between the twelfth-century art of the Khmers, the direct heirs to the previous centuries, and the art of the Renaissance, it must have been due to a reverse process, that is to the importation of oriental objects into Europe.

Let us turn from trying to date the monuments to the question of how long it took to build them. On this topic, too, several extravagant theories have been propounded. If we consider the amount of stone in Angkor Wat in relation to the mechanical means that the Khmers had at their disposal, we are dumbfounded, and we can understand why the Cambodians attributed its construction to Visvarkarman, the divine architect. A former Cambodian Minister of Justice, H. E. Chhun, liked to tell how, at the time of his first trip to Angkor, he tried to calculate the approximate cubic measurement of the stones in Angkor Wat, and figured that constructing the temple could not have taken less than three hundred years! We know now that this is exactly the amount of time it took to build all the great Khmer monuments, not only at

---

4. Prah Khan overgrown. Some lovers of romanticism have reproached the archaeologists of the Ecole Française for denuding the ruins of the vegetation that was destroying them. Many tourists today prefer the monuments, like Prah Khan and Ta Prohm, still overgrown with jungle.

Angkor but throughout the surrounding country. At the rate that H. E. Chhun calculated, it would have taken several thousand years.

Georges Groslier in his pamphlet on Angkor published in 1924 advances a completely opposite hypothesis:

> Contrary to what one might be led to believe by the size and the number of the monuments, the time taken to build them was quite short. Considering the procedure, and because of the distribution of the work and the separate character of each element, a temple could be worked on from every side at the same time, using a large number of labourers. According to calculations that have been minutely worked out, we believe that a brick tower a dozen metres high with a base five metres on a side could have been built in thirty days, and that the building of Angkor Wat could not have taken more than fifty years at the most.

Thanks to recent epigraphic discoveries, we know quite definitely the precise dates of the foundation of the principal temples at Angkor. This tight chronological picture no longer gives us much latitude for guessing. Following the evolution of the decorative and architectural motifs that we can now trace from one monument to another, it has become impossible to think that a building as homogeneous in style as Angkor Wat could have been begun in the middle of the eleventh century at the period of Baphuon, and not finished until the end of the twelfth century, at which time the architecture and decoration were already quite changed. The half century that Georges Groslier allows for the limit of its completion is a maximum which cannot be increased, and which should rather be diminished to the length of Suryavarman II's reign, which lasted thirty years.

The lack of care in construction particularly at the end of the twelfth century is one of the causes of the ruined state of the monuments. The chaotic condition of some of them, for instance Beng Mealea, has sometimes been attributed to a systematic destruction, the consequences of a total war perhaps. I do not think the motive was pure vandalism or religious fanaticism as has sometimes been claimed, because there was another far more simple motive: that is, the search under the pedestals and around the bases of the towers for the sacred relics which always included some gold-leaf and some gems. To reach these relics, robbers did not hesitate to knock over the statues, break the pedestals, set fire when necessary, dig holes in the bases, and split open the stones to get out the T-irons with which they were usually held together. Whether these pillagers were conquering enemies, or simple robbers operating in the abandoned temples, their desecrations explain the interior disorder of the sanctuaries.

Other causes of the deterioration of the monuments were the natural forces which operated silently but all the same effectively. In tropical countries where the climate is wet, an abandoned building laid open to the rain and termites, is promptly overgrown with vegetation and is destined to speedy destruction. Let me again quote a page from *Pèlerin d'Angkor*.

> The fig tree is the ruler of Angkor today. Over the palaces and over the temples which it has patiently pried apart, everywhere it unfolds its smooth pale branches, like the coils of a serpent, and its dome of foliage. At first it was nothing but a small seed carried by the wind to a frieze or to the top of a tower. But as soon as it could germinate it worked its roots like fine threads between the stones, down, down, guided by a sure instinct toward the earth, and when it reached the soil at last, it quickly strengthened and grew with the nourishing sap, until grown enormous, it forced apart, pushed out of line, and split open the walls from top to bottom. The building, defenseless, was destroyed.

One need not imagine an earthquake rocking the country to explain the chaotic condition of some of the monuments, and, anyway, Cambodia is not subject to seismographic disturbances. But the idea of a movement of the foundations, due not to an earthquake but to the settling of the earth, is quite possible. One can clearly see the results of such a process at Angkor Wat where, for instance in the gallery containing the bas-reliefs, all the cross beams which unite the pillars to those of the outer half-vault are cleanly broken off as a result of the sinking of the foundations.

I have now come to the final question which I want to discuss, that is the purpose for which these monuments were intended. I do not hesitate to repudiate the idea that some of them were intended as palaces, princely or royal residences. From the very first, explorers have recognized the essentially religious character of these buildings, completely unsuitable for habitation. Moreover the Chinese Chou Ta Kuen, to whom one must always refer, mentions that the royal and princely residences were covered with tiles either of lead or of clay, which implies that the buildings must have been of light construction, because this type of roofing was never used for brick or stone buildings. Actually at Angkor Thom in the enclosure of Phimeanakas which was once the site of the former royal palace, there is no trace of residences except some foundations intended for wooden structures. There are no remains of these light buildings though a number of them are pictured in the bas-reliefs, so that in studying the archaeological map of the Angkor region, we are seeing only the religious skeleton of the city. Even the enclosing wall is actually the wall of the central temple, the Bayon. But then another question arises: what could have been the purpose of such an accumulation of religious buildings, which finally sapped the vitality of the country like a cancer? For one must realize what bondage they necessitated, and what slavery and taxes their upkeep required.

If, as is generally assumed, these temples were shrines or places of public pilgrimage, one is forced to conclude that their number and size are out of all proportion to the needs of the population, no matter how numerous. One cannot account for this accumulation, nor for the constant construction of additional monuments, with each king trying to outdo the former, culminating in the frenzy of new construction in the twelfth century which saw the successive building of Beng Mealea, Angkor Wat, Banteay Samre, Banteay Kdei, Ta Prohm, Prah Khan, Banteay Chmar, and the Bayon, to mention only the larger ones.

Today we have the key to this puzzle, thanks to recent epigraphic discoveries, and we now know that the ones built by royalty were funerary temples, mausoleums and, to a certain extent, tombs, since royal ashes were inserted into the bases of statues that pictured the deceased in divine form.

The tremendous effort expended in building these royal mausoleums which were at first the distinctive glory of the Khmer Empire, finished by draining all the resources of the kingdom and constituted a principal cause of its decline.

[III]

Personal Cults

VERY few of the innumerable statues of Vishnu and Siva and other gods left to us by the Khmer Empire were idealistic or impersonal representations of these deities. The great majority of them were portraits of kings and princes and high dignitaries, each represented as the god into whom he would be absorbed at the end of his earthly existence.[11]

The names given to the statues, generally a composite of the names of the man and of the god, indicate clearly that men were worshipped as gods.

This system of human cult, though little known inside India itself, was widely practised in outer India. There is evidence that it existed in the ancient Cham kingdom, and in Java and Bali. The fine statues preserved in the Djakarta Museum and in the Dutch museums, originally labelled Vishnu, Siva, and so on, were actually images of dead kings and princes in the guise of Brahman and Buddhist deities.

There is evidence of human cults from the beginning of the Angkor period, and probably they originated even earlier. With the images used in this cult (the term 'image' must be taken in a broad sense because some were of men and some of *lingas*), we have to distinguish between the ones dedicated to the memory of the deceased and the ones of people still living: that is, whether the donor was dedicating the statue to his ancestors or whether he was erecting his own image or an image named after him.

The earliest large group of stone monuments in the Angkor region dates from the ninth century and is dedicated to the funerary cult of the royal family. This group known as Roluos, twenty kilometres south-east of Angkor, includes the three temples of Bakong, Prah Ko, and Lolei. This group shows us how the funerary cult was connected with the worship of the god-king, a subject to which I will return later.

At the same time as King Indravarman installed the god-king at Bakong under the name of Indresvara (Indra [varman] plus -isvara, i.e. Siva), he constructed the six towers of Prah Ko right beside it to shelter the images, in the likeness of Siva and his wife, of his parents, his maternal grandparents and his predecessor, Jayavarman II. At Lolei, in 893, Yasovarman, the son and successor of Indravarman and the founder of Angkor, erected the statues of his parents and his maternal grandparents. All these images have composite names, the first half of which corresponds to the royal title of the deified prince or princess in life, and the second half is either -isvara or -devi, according to the sex.

In the following century King Rajendravarman consecrated the monuments known as Mebon Oriental, 952, and Pre Rup, 961, in honour of his parents.

At the end of the twelfth century, in 1186, Jayavarman VII constructed Ta Prohm to shelter the statue of his mother and her spiritual master. In 1191 he built Prah Khan for the statue of his father.

Later we have the clear example of the big stele at Phimeanakas, according to which Queen Jayarajadevi, wife of Jayavarman VII, 'put up many statues all over of her father, mother, brothers, friends and relations, known to her personally or by name only.' In the same way her older sister, after the queen's death, 'erected numerous images of Sri Jayarajadevi, along with images of the king himself, in all the cities.' We also know quite definitely that many statues put up by Jayavarman VII were mostly the likenesses of princes or of deified dignitaries whose names we can read carved on the doors of the chapels.

Visitors to Angkor must have noticed some of the inscriptions on the buildings.[12] With very few exceptions the idols described in these inscriptions at the entrances to the sanctuaries carry the title of *kamrateng jagat* or 'lord of the universe'. In the pre-Angkor era and during the first part of the Angkor period up to the latter part of the tenth century, the gods were given the same title as the king, the princes and all high dignitaries, that is *kamrateng anh* which means 'my lord'. During the second half of the tenth century the title given to the statues of gods impersonating human beings was changed to *kamrateng jagat*. This epithet was preferred because it clearly established the distinction that was needed when the custom of putting up funerary statues of royalty became general. Then an elevation, usually, but not always, posthumous, could be conferred on a prince or a dignitary, promoting him from *kamrateng anh* to *kamrateng jagat*, in the form of a statue with the attributes of a god.

In an inscription at Banteay Chmar we find a text conferring the honours of apotheosis on four brave soldiers who died defending a prince, the son of Jayavarman VII. The inscription is really a decree of their canonization. The abbreviated text follows:

When the traitor Bharata Rahu wanted to take over the royal palace, all the troops guarding the capital fled. The prince entered into combat. The *sanjak* Arjuna and the *sanjak* Sri Dharadevapura fought to defend him, and were killed before him. The prince gave Bharata Rahu a blow on the nose and knocked him over. Afterwards the title of *amteng* was ordered to be bestowed on the two *sanjaks* and statues of them were erected. The prince also bestowed riches and honours on their families. . . .

Another time the prince went to the country of the Chams. He captured a fortress built by the Cham king, and retreated. Just then the advance guard of the Cham army, taking a short cut, surprised the rear guard of the Khmers. The prince brought his troops forward again to come to their aid. He took up a position on top of a knoll, just as the Chams rallied their forces for an assault. The rear guard of the Khmers was forced back. Only thirty of them survived. The prince advanced, fighting on to the foot of the hill. The Chams encircled him, and none of his men dared to come to his defense. The *sanjak* Sri Deva and the *sanjak* Sri Vardhana, bound by an oath of loyalty, fought their way to the prince. They threw themselves in front of him and attacked the Chams who pushed forward in great numbers, and finally they were knocked down, having nothing left to fight with but their hands. Attacked by the Cham arrows, and wounded in the belly, they died true to their oath. The prince ordered a royal ceremony in their honour. After that the Khmer army which he led in seventy-eight different engagements protected him resolutely. When he returned to Kambuja, he deigned to confer the title of *amteng* on the two *sanjaks*, and he had their statues erected.

These statues were placed in the four corners of the main sanctuary at Banteay Chmar, in the centre of which was the statue of the prince who had himself been divinized by proclamation of his father, Jayavarman VII.

Of the images of *kamrateng jagat* dating from this reign, some are single, others are in groups of three. In

the instance at Prah Khan already quoted we find three
chapels all in a line in one court, containing three statues
representing the father, the mother, and the son. A similar instance is found in another inscription according to
which a trio of statues represent the spiritual master and
the father and mother of the builder. Most of the groups
of three statues in museum collections represent Buddha
seated below Naga, between Lokesvara and the female
figure, Prajnaparamita. Sometimes this order is inverted.

Most of the single statues in the monuments that have
been studied represent divinities in the form of Lokesvara,
the compassionate Bodhisattva, or of Prajnaparamita,
the Perfection of Wisdom, recognizable because she
carries a miniature Buddha on the front of her headdress.

The type of worship that can be discerned from the
titles of the statues indicates a remarkable religious syn-
cretism. Buddhist images are found next to statues of
Vishnu and Siva, and it is often difficult to determine what
religion inspired any particular image or triad. Also, this
religion was essentially a worship of human beings and
this feature necessitated the inscriptions at the entrances
to the chapels. An image of Vishnu or Buddha or
Lokesvara would be recognized without having to be
named, but an inscription was needed to point out the
likeness of an individual who might not be particularly
associated with the god portrayed. There was also the
understandable interest of the donors in having their
names recorded, thus in many instances revealing to us
the special significance of the statues.

By erecting an idol, a *kamrateng jagat*, or 'lord of the
universe', which was the 'holy image' (*vrah rupa*) of a
king or a prince or a dignitary, and calling it by his name,
the Khmers thought they could perpetuate in stone

the essence of the person they wanted to worship.

'And if in accordance with some ancient Indian sagas', Foucher wrote, 'they believed that a person's individuality was contained in his name and his form, one can see that this procedure would accomplish true deification.'[13]

Epigraphy gives us some clues as to the concepts which were behind this cult of eminent men, a cult which I repeat was as much Hindu as it was Buddhist, and which was not even entirely funerary, since it often consisted in erecting statues of people still living.[14]

We find these clues in the final lines of the inscriptions in which the kings exhort their descendants to carry on the cult and to maintain the temple entrusted to their care. The words sometimes have a tone of vehement supplication, almost tragic, which indicates how seriously they were concerned with their life after death.

'Guard this *dharma* which for me is like a bridge', begs King Yasovarman, recommending to his successors the maintenance of Lolei, in which he had erected statues of his parents. And King Rajendravarman writes in the inscription at Pre Rup: 'They claim correctly that supplication is the death of kings, as it has for a goal the fulfilment of their wishes. But what I proffer, out of a passion for *dharma*, and having only the well-being of this *dharma* in mind, is that this supplication is for the immortality one should try to achieve.'

What is this *dharma* whose continuance is to be assured by the maintenance of the monuments and devotion to the cult? A series of epigraphic texts which cannot be examined in detail here indicates that in these inscriptions, *dharma*, literally meaning 'law' or 'religion', also connotes 'establishment of royal authority' or 'sacred

establishment' designed to create this authority and assure
its perpetuity.

As stated in one of the above inscriptions this procedure
is truly a 'bridge' by which the builder is united on the
one hand with his forebears, whose statues he consecrates,
and on the other hand with his descendants to whom he
confides the care of his monuments and the worship of
the family cult.

In Indian religions an image cannot be worshipped unless it is 'alive', that is, animated by the spirit of the god,
and the ritual of consecration bringing it to life consists of
opening the eyes of the statue, or of the mask sculptured on
the *linga*, by the symbolic act of piercing them with a
pin. In some countries, notably Tibet, Buddhist statues
are 'animated' by the insertion of a formula, a few words
from the holy scriptures, into the base. This formula is a
substitute for the body of Buddha, whose relics are inserted in the great *stupas*.

We know that in Cambodia images of living persons
were supposed to contain their 'essence', that is their 'vital
principle'. But when death removed this principle from
their bodies, how were the images to remain animated?
When a king consecrated the image of someone already
dead, there must have been some rite by which he could
impart life to it which was essential to the cult. The
Javanese and Balinese had such rites symbolizing the ani-
mation of statues after death.[15] The final step in these
rites was enclosing the statue in a tomb, or more correctly
a funerary temple.

---

5.   Ta Som overgrown. 'The fig tree is the ruler of Angkor today. Over
the palaces and over the temples which it has patiently pried apart,
everywhere it unfolds its smooth pale branches, and its dome of foliage.'
Pierre Loti.

We must remember that in India, whose religious ideas formed the basis for those of the Khmers as well as for those of the Javanese and the Balinese, the tomb (if there was one instead of cremation and immersion of the ashes) did not have the same meaning as in the West. I refer to the description of a *stupa* in Paul Mus's book on Borobodur. 'We have before us a sepulchre which is also in fact, a temple. It is a sanctuary tomb. ... The tomb becomes not so much a shelter for the dead, as a kind of new architectural body, substituted for the mortal remains of a deceased "cosmic man" where his magic soul will live on and prolong his existence. The temple is a new body, an architectural one, which may be thought of as the house of the dead, but only in the same way that his body lived in it while still alive.'

This is exactly the concept of the statue which was a likeness in stone, this 'body of glory' which bears the same name as the *stupa*, a 'tomb that has life in it', animated like the statue with the *dharma* of the former king.

The indispensable role of these statues explains the care which kings and other eminent people took to assure their continued cult. It explains why the statues were erected in buildings of great permanence, as well as the pomp of the rituals and the supplications addressed to the coming generations.

The cult of the Devaraja, or god-king, is closely interwoven with the beliefs I have just mentioned. In the Hinduized kingdoms of Indochina and Indonesia, Hinduistic cults especially of Siva accentuated a tendency already apparent in India itself and developed into the

---

6. Baksei Chamkrong, a classic pyramid temple built in 947, with mounting layers of decreasing size, and similarly proportioned steps diminishing in number and height.

cult of royalty. The royal essence, or as referred to in
several texts, the 'inner self', was supposed to reside in
a *linga* ensconced in a pyramid in the exact centre of the
royal city which in turn was located in the centre of the
world. This miraculous *linga*, a kind of palladium of the
kingdom, was supposed to have been obtained from Siva
through an intermediary who was a Brahman priest, who
then gave it to the first king of the dynasty. This communion between the king and the god through the mediation of a priest took place on the sacred mountain located in the centre of the capital.[16]

In Cambodia the solemn installation of this royal cult
was celebrated early in the ninth century by Jayavarman
II, the first king of the Angkorian dynasty. It took place
on the summit of Phnom Kulen. We know that his successor, Indravarman, instituted the cult of the god-king
at Bakong under the name of Indresvara. The builder of
the first temple of Angkor, Yasovarman, installed the cult
at the summit of Phnom Bakheng at the centre of the city
under the name of Yasodharesvara, about 900. The royal
god was transferred in 921 by King Jayavarman IV to
Koh Ker, the short-lived capital. This national god, at
the summit of the great central pyramid, was called by
the name of *kamrateng jagat ta rajya*, 'lord of the universe who is royalty'. After the god-king was returned to
Angkor, it was installed on Phimeanakas, which had been
especially constructed at the beginning of the eleventh
century. At the end of the eleventh century Baphuon was
constructed to house the golden *linga* containing the
'inner self' of King Udayadityavarman II. After the
adoption of Buddhism in the second half of the twelfth
century, the god-king left his *linga* to enter into the statue
of Buddha. Jayavarman VII built the Bayon to shelter

the statue of the Buddha-king in the centre of the city of Angkor which had been rebuilt through his efforts.

From all this evidence it is safe to say that it was the king who was the great god of ancient Cambodia, the one to whom the biggest groups of monuments and all the temples in the form of mountains were dedicated. At the summit of the mountain located at the centre of the city as well as at the centre of the universe, the king, embodied in his own sacred image, entered into contact with the world of the gods.

The national temple was also the personal temple of the king, erected by him during his life. When after his death his ashes or mortal remains were deposited there to animate the idol and give the cult a living image, the temple became his mausoleum, while his successor built another sanctuary for the god-king. This was the theoretical sequence at least, but only the most powerful of the Khmer rulers were able to erect these temples, which even today are the pride of the ancient capital. The kings who had short reigns, or who were troubled with revolutions, had neither the time nor the resources to build temples for the god-king, or in other words, their own mausoleums.

Angkor Wat can be called a sanctuary to Vishnu, but the Vishnu worshipped there is not the ancient god Vishnu, nor any of the forms of his traditional incarnations, but King Suryavarman II, identified with Vishnu after his death, embodied in him and living in this mausoleum —so beautifully decorated with graceful *apsaras*—much like Vishnu in his celestial palace.

In the form of man the king lived in a palace built of wood and other light materials, but in the form of a god he resided in a palace of stone. The great Khmer temples were not products of a popular faith, like our cathedrals. They were princely buildings for the worship of kings and members of their entourage, deified in the form of one of the Hindu or Buddhist gods. It would be a serious mistake to think of these temples as similar to a modern church or a pagoda. If the people were sometimes admitted to them on great occasions, it was not to offer prayers or sacrifices for divine mercy, but rather to prostrate themselves before the image of the god-king or the Buddha-king or other deified dignitaries.

Buddhism of the Lesser Vehicle, which was fundamentally antipathetic to the conception of individual personality and which even went so far as to deny its existence, could not but destroy the flowering of such an aristocratic cult, which gathered together the people only for the purpose of worshipping the god-king and his great chiefs. Perhaps this was one of the causes of the rapid decline of the Khmer Empire in the thirteenth and fourteenth centuries. From the time that the sovereign ceased to be Siva descended to earth, or the living Buddha like Jayavarman VII, the kings ceased to inspire the supreme religious respect which had enabled them to be such powerful rulers. Undermined by the spirit of Singhalese Buddhism, the prestige of the king diminished, his temporal power crumbled. The god-king was knocked down from his altar, and it was the twilight of both gods and kings.

However, the tradition of a personal cult was so deeply rooted in the court that even when Singhalese Buddhism became the official religion, it was to bow to the magic influence of the cult, and still continues to do so. In the Wat Prah Keo at Phnom Penh, better known among westerners as the Silver Pagoda, at the foot of the altar there is a gold statue of a standing Buddha, studded with diamonds. To the unknowing visitor it looks like any other of the many statues of Buddha, though perhaps more costly. But if one realizes that it was made from the melted jewelry of King Norodom and that its measurements are exactly those of the deceased ruler, one has to admit its relation to the statues of *kamrateng jagat* that inhabit the ancient temples of Angkor.

[IV]

Temples or Tombs

I<small>N</small> the previous chapter we have examined the evidence to prove that 'animated' images of the Khmer kings in the guise of gods were placed in their monuments, and that in fact the great kings of Angkor built the monuments in order to contain their images and perpetuate their personal cults.

There has been a prolonged academic discussion among the scholars of the first part of this century as to whether the monuments should be called temples or tombs. At first they were considered to be temples.

In 1933 Jean Przyluski formulated an hypothesis, which seemed quite daring at the time, that Angkor Wat was the tomb of Suryavarman II.[17] Based on the fact that the building faced west instead of east as the other Khmer temples did, and that the story of the bas-reliefs along the length of the second-level gallery ran in the customary direction of a funeral procession, that is, keeping the left side toward the monument, Przyluski concluded that Angkor Wat was an entirely different type of building from the others. It was not a temple in which the divine cult of a god was celebrated, consisting of auspicious rites performed with the right hand, but a sepulchre in which a dead man was honoured with a funerary cult, calling for inauspicious rites, performed with the left hand.

I argued against this theory, not because I refused to believe that Angkor Wat had a funerary significance, a connexion I had myself recognized twenty years before, but because I refused to concede that Angkor was basically different from the other Khmer monuments. In 1933, I wrote:

> What we have here is not an orientation suggesting funerary rites, but a well-known architectural arrangement and plan, that cannot denote anything but a temple. If one thinks of the word 'temple' as I do, not as a place of worship, but as the house of a god, to refuse Angkor this appellation is to deny the evidence.
>
> I concede that the presence of skeletons and ashes would explain why the monument faces toward the west, but I refuse to believe that Angkor was only a sepulchre, like the Chinese sepulchres. It is a tomb, in the sense of the resting place of a king after death, but precisely because a Khmer king 'went to heaven' at his death, this was his habitation in the form of a celestial palace in the centre of which was placed an image of the god with whom the king was identified.

The problem revolved around the question of what was done with the mortal remains of the kings after death. Certainly if corpses, including that of the king, were burned and the ashes scattered in the river or in the sea, as is the custom in India today, it would be quite incorrect to call the monuments tombs. But if the corpse was interred, or if as in Cambodia or Thailand today, the ashes or skeleton were enclosed in an urn after cremation and this urn was deposited in a pagoda, then it was legitimate to ask whether certain monuments did not serve as mausoleums for the mortal remains of kings and princes.

There is unfortunately not much to be learned about this question from Chinese sources. At the end of the thirteenth century, Chou Ta Kuen says, 'The ruler is interred in a tower, but I am not sure whether they bury his body, or only his bones.'

Unfortunately the monuments of Angkor were all subjected at one time or another to systematic plundering. The robbers have not left a single sanctuary intact. They did not hesitate to knock over the idols and to break open the enormous monolithic pedestals to reach the 'treasure', which was placed in a deep pit under the central sanctuary of the pyramids, or to knock off the tops of the towers to get access to the deposits hidden in their summits. Thus it is very difficult to know what was ceremonially placed in the concealed cavities in the numerous honeycombed deposit stones found in the ruins, and especially whether any of them contained human remains. Fragments of gold, rough gems, an enormous tektite* have been found among the ruins but never *in situ* in the hollowed deposit stones.

In Java another method of disposing of the dead which was similar to a pre-Hindu custom and which persisted to the height of the Indo-Javanese period, was traditional. In several places oval or ellipsoidal tubs have been found, which were at first taken for bath tubs, but which later were found to be sarcophagi. Of the two tubs on which I have some details, one has an outlet hole in the bottom, the other is decorated on the outside with death heads resting on crescent moons. The two tubs are similar in their shape and size; one is $1.78 \times .87 \times .60$ metres, the other is $1.67 \times 1.06 \times .78$ metres.

* natural glass of meteoric origin, bottle green and usually translucent.

7. The Baphuon under renovation by the Service de Conservation. This pyramid temple was built at the end of the eleventh century to contain the golden *linga* which represented the royal essence of Udayadityavarman. The inner core of this, and all the pyramid-temples, was merely a pile of rubble.

In recent years the work of the Conservation Service at Angkor has brought to light a dozen stone tubs. One of them at Banteay Samre is complete with lid. All except one, that still have the base intact, have an outlet hole in the bottom, like the Javanese sarcophagi.

All the tubs were empty when found, and not one of them was found truly *in situ*. Even the ones at Phnom Bakeng and at Angkor Wat, which were dug up during the excavations of the central sanctuaries, had been displaced and tampered with by the treasure seekers.

Probably, like the Javanese tubs, they are sarcophagi. Although the small dimensions of most of them do not seem suited to this purpose, we should remember that their capacity is not very different from the contemporary urns used to contain the corpses, in a kneeling position, of Cambodian and Siamese kings and princes, 1.20 metres in height and .60 metres in diameter. Furthermore, the general shape of these tubs, particularly the one that is complete with lid, recalls vividly the form of some of the Cambodian and Siamese coffins that have a pyramidal lid. The mask of Rahu decorating the mouth of the outlet is not the only similarity between them.

The outlet hole that we find on each one that still has its base could have served to run off the liquid that would have come from a fresh cadaver, just as in the urns and the biers that are used in Cambodia and Thailand today to store the body before its cremation. The hole in the top of the only tub which still has a lid could have served

---

8. Mukhalinga, National Museum, Phnom Penh. The cult of the god-king, whose 'royal essence' was supposed to reside in a *linga* ensconced in a pyramid in the exact centre of the royal city, was first introduced by Jayavarman II in the ninth century. Later, with the introduction of Buddhism, the god-king became an image of the king as Buddha.

to let out the gases, or to insert the white thread or the
white cloth which is still used in present-day ceremonies
as a symbolic connexion between the dead and the living.
By analogy with funeral customs of today, therefore, one
might suppose that these sarcophagi served to dry out
the corpses. Then after the dessicated remains were burned and the ashes placed in a reliquary, the sarcophagus
would have been buried in the funerary temple consecrated to the deceased, for lack of any more appropriate
place to preserve this appurtenance of the dead.

Another possibility is that the tubs were made to contain corpses already dessicated. The hole in the lid and
the outlet in the base were provided for the periodic
ablution of the mortal remains, a ritual that still survives
in the modern Laotian custom of running a stream of
water over the sarcophagus urn of a *bonze* (monk) or
prince. Whatever was done in Khmer funeral rites, we
know that sarcophagi were frequently deposited in the
monuments. This does not exclude the possibility that
in other monuments ashes were deposited in the base of
the statue, because in Cambodia sarcophagi have only
been found in a few of the larger temples.

We must conclude that the monuments that date from
the time of Jayavarman VII were temples as well as tombs
because they enclosed divine images, and even though
the cult practised there was funerary, in the sense that
it was directed to people who were deceased, it was also
divine since the images worshipped were Devas and
Bodhisattvas. Angkor Wat was the final habitation of a
being who enjoyed certain divine prerogatives during his
life, and whom death had transformed into a god. It was
a 'funerary temple'.

[V]

Architectural Symbolism

FROM my very first contact with the Angkor monuments in 1912, I was struck with the symbolism implicit in this architecture. The Khmer architects seemed to have been guided by concepts which at that time we were only on the threshold of understanding.

Since then research has enabled us to perceive how the architectural symbolism of the ancient Khmers reflected their belief in an intimate relationship between the universe and the earth. Here is what Professor Robert von Heine-Geldern wrote in his fine article 'Weltbild und Bauform in Südostasien'.[18]

> The effect of cosmology on architecture in the civilized countries of Indochina and Indonesia has already been noted by various scholars, but its true importance as the inspiration of all Hindu colonial architecture has not been fully realized. This connexion was based on a conception of the world which originated in the ancient Orient, the belief in a magic relation between microcosm and macrocosm, between the human world and the universe, between terrestrial manifestations on the one hand and the points of the compass and the constellations on the other. According to this belief, elements, colours, animals, plants, stones, metals, the parts of the body, personality, every occurrence, age and sex, asceticism and indulgence, birth and death, all had their allotted place in space, and were controlled by the stars. Consequently each thing had its 'magic position' in the structure of the universe, and its 'magic moment', which was related to the motion of the planets. Humanity was forever in the control of cosmic

forces. This concept was applied to social groups even more than to individuals. Kingdom, city, monastery, nothing could prosper unless it was in harmony with these universal forces. In order to achieve this harmony, men tried to build the kingdom, the capital, the palace, the temple, in the form of microcosms, which were the replicas of the structure of the macrocosm. They tried to integrate all things in this setting according to space and time. They attempted to bring the court, the government, provincial divisions, measures, weights, currencies, customs, and activities into conformity with the laws of nature.

This concept was precisely the inspiration for the great architectural creations of the Khmers. Angkor Wat with its wall and moats, its central sanctuary, its entrances, its pyramidal temples and its bridges with *naga* balustrades, as well as other complicated monuments such as Neak Pean or the Bayon, are actually representations in stone of the great myths of Hindu cosmology. The purpose of this system was to reproduce on earth a terrestrial model of all or part of the heavenly world, thus ensuring that intimate harmony between the two worlds without which humanity could not prosper.

Let us look for instance at the city of Angkor Thom, the capital of the kingdom which Jayavarman VII restored in the last decades of the twelfth century. Unlike our western cities, it was not just a group of houses, a market, and a seat of government. It was a replica in miniature of the fabled world of Hindu cosmology, a small model of the universe, a microcosm.

According to Brahman ideas the world consisted of a central continent, Jambudvipa, with Meru, the cosmic mountain, rising at its centre. This continent was encircled by six concentric rings of land, separated by seven oceans, the outer one of which was enclosed by a rock wall. At the summit of Meru was the city of Brahma, the home of the gods, surrounded by the eight guardians of the cardinal points.

The Buddhist system is different enough in detail, though it too is based on the idea of a central mountain, Meru, on top of which rise the various layers of the heavens. Meru is surrounded by seven circular and concentric chains of mountains, separated by as many oceans. Beyond them is the great ocean, containing the four island-continents, one in each of the four regions of space. The region at the south is Jambudvipa, the land of men. This universe, like the Brahman universe, is surrounded by a huge wall of rock. At the summit of Meru is the residence of the four rulers of the cardinal points. Indra sits at the top surrounded by the thirty-three gods. Over Indra are the layers of the sky, varying in number according to the sect and the era.

These two systems are alike in their idea of a central mountain, the pivot of the world, which is bounded by a high wall beyond which is the ocean.

Obviously the Hindu and Cambodian city-makers did not attempt to reproduce this system in all its detail. Magic, and especially oriental magic, was content with an approximation. The essentials were the central temple of the city as the magic mountain, the enclosing wall as the wall of rock, and beyond, the moat filled with water as the ocean. The microcosm is a familiar symbol in their literature, a frequently recurring concept, used and abused by Hindu poets as well as by the composers of the Sanskrit inscriptions on the Cambodian temple walls.

In the eleventh century when Udayadityavarman II constructed the Baphuon which was at the centre of a city antedating Angkor Thom, he did it, says a stele found at the foot of the monument, 'because he thought that the centre of the universe was marked by Meru, and he thought it fitting to have a Meru in the centre of his capital.'

The terms 'central mountain', 'mountain of gold', or 'horn of gold'—which were the contemporary epithets for Meru, the cosmic mountain at the centre of the universe—became technical terms to designate the central temple of the capital. The architectural form adopted for this sacrosanct monument emphasized the identification. It was a mountain in the form of a pyramid. The oldest example that we can be certain was intended to be a replica of Meru was Bakong, constructed in 881 to mark the centre of Hariharalaya, the capital at that time. Numerous monuments repeated the same form: Phnom Bakheng, a temple-pyramid built on the summit of a natural mountain marking the centre of the first city of Angkor; Koh Ker, the short-lived capital of Jayavarman IV; Phimeanakas of Jayavarman V; Baphuon of Udayadityavarman II. Later the same form was used for many great temples, which, even though they were not at the centre of the capital, were royal mausoleums: Mebon, Pre Rup, Takeo, Angkor Wat.

Moreover the association of a temple with a mountain fits well with the concept of the ancient Khmers, like that of the Hindus, regarding their place of cult. A Khmer *prasat* was not like a modern Buddhist pagoda, a gathering place where the religious went through their acts of devotion and where the laity came periodically to listen to the exposition of the law. It was the habitation of a god, the replica of a celestial palace or of one of those high places where gods were pleased to live.

The simple tower of brick of pre-Angkorian times,

composed of mounting levels of diminishing size, already gave the clear impression of a mountain top rising into the sky, with a cap of stone or bronze embellishing the pinnacle. This created a very different impression from a Greek temple, for instance. Sometimes the pyramidal form was topped with a quincunx of towers, in imitation of Mount Meru which was supposed to have had five peaks. Concerning the pyramidal temple Mebon Oriental, an inscription says, 'In the middle of this sea, which is the sacred pool of Yasodhara, he erected a mountain, with a summit like that of Meru, covered with temples and sanctuaries plastered in stucco.'

In the treatises on Hindu architecture and inscriptions, the different types of pyramidal monuments are called by a variety of names, but all of them mean the same thing, 'jewel decorating the head'. This was a gem placed in the middle of the forehead or on the headdress which was, as we know, a customary part of the adornment of a rajah. This name emphasizes the role of the temple, which, even though it might be on one level, fulfilled the function of a 'high place' where the world of men could communicate with the world of gods. In Chapter III, I have explained how the god-king or the royal *linga*, containing the essence of royalty, was sent down by Siva himself, through a Brahman intermediary, to the king who founded the royal dynasty. This communion between the king and the god, through the mediation of the royal chaplain, which took place first on the sacred mountain, was daily re-enacted in the temple at the centre of the capital. Just as Mount Meru was supposed to penetrate to the celestial vault and to carry the lowest layer of the heavens on its peak, in the same way the central temple of the city established the liaison between men and gods through the mediation of the god on earth, who was the king.

This was the same function as was performed in Meso-potamia by the *zikkurat*, the most famous example of which was the Babylonian 'Tower of Babel', the 'gateway to the sky', which was not just a myth but a real tower, and which was supposed to permit men to enter into heaven. This famous tower, according to Herodotus and other ancient writers, had a subterranean part that ex-tended as far into the earth as the visible part rose in the sky. In the same way in Indian cosmology, Mount Meru extended under the earth and even under the sea, because the axis of the universe had to be rooted in the under-world. That was what the sculptors of the bas-reliefs at the Bayon wanted to represent by covering the base of Mount Meru with a gigantic fish, a symbol of the ocean.

Their effort to reproduce the subterranean part of Mount Meru architecturally in stone and on a human scale led the Khmer builders to cover over the carved bases of their towers in many instances by a second layer of stone similarly decorated. This double layer for which there is no other logical explanation is clearly visible at the base of the central tower of the Baphuon, which as I have said was supposed to be a small replica of Meru. The same architectural symbol is found in Java at Boro-bodur, where the lowest terrace decorated with a series of bas-reliefs of the underworld, the world of desire and sensual pleasures, has been purposely covered over.

Perhaps it was the same idea, carried out in a some-what different way, which motivated the builders of the

9. Banteay Srei, portal to the main sanctuary, built in the second half of the tenth century. This tiny 'citadel of women', finely carved of pink sandstone, and remarkably well preserved, is one of the most perfect of the Khmer monuments.

Terrace of the Leper King. This structure, which has a receding shape, and which is decorated with bands of bas-reliefs, one on top of another, depicting fabulous creatures such as Naga, Garuda, and Kumbhanda, who frequented the slopes of Meru, is certainly a replica of the magic mountain. And we know that the outer wall is duplicated on the inside with a second inner wall decorated with analogous scenes, but representing demoniac creatures, recognizable by their frowning brows and the fangs at the corners of their mouths. These interior bas-reliefs, intended to remain invisible, almost certainly represented creatures who were supposed to haunt the subterranean slopes of Meru.[19] Instead of burying these bas-reliefs underground, the sculptors built them above ground and then covered them with an outer layer, in the same way that they masked the bases of the towers at the Baphuon with a second outer base.

Thus we have in the central mountain of the city a representation in human scale of the mountain which is the axis of the world. That is the first requirement of a microcosm. The two other essential elements, the ocean, and the wall of rock encircling the universe, are represented by the moat and the enclosing wall. A Sanskrit poem begins, 'The city is enclosed in immense walls like the mountains that girdle the great world. There, contemplating the mounting gold and silver terraces, the inhabitants have no need to wish they could see the peaks of Meru and Kailasa.'

This tradition was still so much alive at the time when Angkor was restored by Jayavarman VII that the inscriptions he had placed at the four corners of the city compare

---

10. Banteay Srei, niche, tenth century.

the wall to the chain of mountains enclosing the universe, and the surrounding moat to the ocean. 'The first pierced the brilliant sky with its pinnacle, the other reached down to the unplumbed depths of the world of serpents. This mountain of victory and this ocean of victory built by the king, simulated the arc of his great glory.'

Even today a modern city like Phnom Penh, which has neither walls nor a moat, is traditionally thought of as a microcosm, as evidenced by the fact that the king, on the day of his consecration as King of Cambodia, takes possession of the city by marching around it in imitation of the legendary king who took possession of the world by encircling it on the outermost shore next to the outer ocean. The cosmic character of his royal promenade is further emphasized by the fact that the king makes use of four successive types of transport and changes his headdress four times, each time assuming the traditional costume and the mount of one of the kings of the four cardinal points.

In Hindu cosmology the bridge between men and the gods is represented by a rainbow. Paul Mus was able to prove, by finding several corroborating clues, that the bridge with *naga* balustrades which formed a passage over the moat from the world of men to the royal city was an image of the rainbow.[20]

All over East Asia and India, the rainbow is compared to a multi-coloured serpent rearing its head in the sky or drinking water from the sea. The myths sometimes speak of two serpents, since there is quite frequently a double rainbow. Probably it was the double rainbow marking out a divine path to the sky which inspired the use of *naga* balustrades on each side of the bridges, an earthly representation of that divine path.

We know that in modern symbolism the staircase made of gold, or silver, or crystal, or according to some texts a stair of seven colours, by which Buddha was supposed to have descended from the heaven of the thirty-third station to the summit of Meru to preach the Law to his mother, this rainbow stair is also represented by a ladder whose sides are formed of *naga*s.

At Angkor Thom as at Prah Khan and at Banteay Chmar, the bridge with *naga* balustrades, found in Khmer art from the ninth century on, is enhanced by various elements which emphasize its symbol as a rainbow and add a second symbolism even more curious than the first. These bridges lead to the gates of the city which reproduce, at the four cardinal points in a reduced form, the aspect of the temple itself. They represent the extension and projection of the royal power emanating from the temple in the four cardinal directions. These doors at Angkor Thom have giant three-headed elephants in the angles formed by their façades, on which are seated figures of Indra, the wielder of thunderbolts and the master of the thirty-third heaven. Thus the rainbow is also the bow of Indra; it is even called by that name in present-day Cambodia. This representation of the god Indra at the end of the bridge accentuates the fact that the bridge with the *naga* balustrades is symbolic of the rainbow ladder.

But there is more. The long rows of gods and giants holding the *naga*s are not just a whim of the sculptor. They are certainly meant to recall the myth of the churning of the sea, having the three necessary elements for this operation: the ocean represented by the moat of the city, the pivoting mountain represented by the tower over the gate, and the *naga* balustrade representing the cosmic

serpent with which the gods pivoted the mountain, as if
with a rope, in order to extract the liquid of immortality.
The sculptors could be sure that by adding the double
row of gods and giants to the combination of the moat-
gate-*naga*, the myth of the churning of the sea of milk
would be clearly indicated.

By creating the symbol of the churning at the gates
of his capital, King Jayavarman VII further established
its divinity. In addition a much repeated literary theme,
commonly used by the court poets, compared the churning to a great battle from which the king extracted good
fortune and victory. From this accumulation of symbolism
it is easy to see that the churning of the sea by the pivoting mountain represented a magic operation which
assured the nation of victory and prosperity.

As we have just seen, from the ninth century on, the
rainbow was successfully transformed into a functional
element of architecture as a bridge with *naga* balustrades.
At the same epoch and even earlier the motif of the rainbow as a span between the human world and the world
of the gods was employed by Khmer artists on bas-reliefs
on the lintels of doorways to the sanctuaries. Instead of
greeting the visitor outside the temple and leading him
to the divine residence by the rainbow bridge with a *naga*
balustrade, the rainbow-shaped design was placed on the
lintel over the chapel entrance. The act of passing
through, under the lintel, was sufficient to symbolize the
transition from one world to the other. Frequently the
small figure of Indra was added in the centre of the bow,
sometimes seated on a three-headed elephant, sometimes
on the head of a lion similar to those on Javanese
designs.[21] The presence of Indra confirmed that the bow-
shaped design was a rainbow and the building a *prasat*.

The significance of the design on the lintel, which was not only a functional element of architecture but also a symbolic motif, leads me to mention some other symbolic motifs frequently used by the builders.

The central section of the Elephant Terrace in front of the eastern entrance of the Royal Palace, in the same line with the Gate of Victory and Phimeanakas, is decorated by great standing *garudas* with lifted wings. They are in the form of caryatids which were supposed to support a royal pavilion built of light materials which stood in the centre of the terrace. Now if we examine the bas-reliefs at Angkor Wat in the gallery picturing heaven and the underworld, we see that the celestial palaces are held aloft by *garudas* and by lions. Most probably these *garuda* caryatids were supposed to indicate that the palaces were floating in the heavens, just like the imagined celestial palaces of the gods.

The terrace which leads to Prah Khan at Kompong Thom is decorated with *hamsas*, or sacred geese, flying with wings outspread. Here again the symbolism is clear. The flying chariot of the god of riches, which had been stolen from him by the demon Ravana, is always described as borne on the wings of *hamsas*. We can surmise that the building of light materials constructed over these friezes was identified with that chariot which was so often pictured on the bas-reliefs.

The bas-reliefs themselves were not just decorations to enliven the flat walls, and the scenes that were pictured were not only reminiscent of the events portrayed. The magic power of these images of the gods transformed the building into a celestial dwelling. The figures of dancing *apsaras* decorating the walls of Angkor Wat were not only to please the eye. Their purpose was to transform this severe stone abode into a heavenly palace.

The same was true of the traditional mythological scenes sculptured on the pediments and also of the long bas-reliefs decorating the galleries of Angkor Wat, the Bayon, and Banteay Chmar. To think of them as purely aesthetic in their appeal would be a great mistake. Just as a statue made according to the requirements and duly consecrated by the proper rites could become the god himself, so a bas-relief picturing a god in a certain legendary episode could contribute to the magic life of the temple. That is why one finds scenes carefully sculptured in obscure and inaccessible places where they are not even visible. They were not made to please the eye of a visitor or to instruct him, but to materialize on earth the world of the gods. This is also true of the historical bas-reliefs at Angkor Wat and the Bayon. The bas-relief of Suryavarman II surrounded by his court at Angkor Wat, and the bas-reliefs of episodes from the life of Jayavarman VII at the Bayon were intended to animate these buildings with the actual living presence of these two kings.[22]

Neak Pean, a unique monument built by Jayavarman VII, is another example of the most complete architectural symbolism. Tourists have a vague idea that because of its pools and fountains, it was a kind of watering place that had healing powers for pilgrims. But very few visitors know that in all probability it was an elaborate method of installing some hot springs symbolizing Lake Anavatapta in the high Himalayas, a lake sacred to Buddhism.

Neak Pean has a small central sanctuary forming a little island with steps leading from the front down to the square pool that surrounds it. The bodies of two dragons form the edge of the island, and their intertwined tails join in a decoration at the back. The modern Cambodian name of the monument, *prea-sat neac pon*, means the 'tower of the intertwined dragons'. Tangent to the central pool are four smaller pools in which the water must have been at a lower level. The water poured from the central pool into the surrounding pools through four fountain-heads in the form of a lion, an elephant, a horse, and a man.

According to Buddhist literature, Lake Anavatapta was fed by hot springs and was sacred because of its heal-ing powers. Buddhas, Bodhisattvas, saints, and hermits, as well as afflicted people, came to bathe in it. The springs flowed through fountain-heads in the form of a lion, an elephant, a horse, and a bull. At Neak Pean the fourth fountain-head is a man instead of a bull. But there is lit-tle doubt that it was intended to be a symbolic repre-sentation of the sacred lake.

I hope I have made it clear by these explanations that the arrangement of a Khmer city and its architecture and decoration were governed by a whole series of magic and religious beliefs, and not determined by utilitarian or aesthetic aims. To understand these monuments one has to be acquainted with the mythological images on which they were modelled. The builders' genius lay in creating beautiful structures within the rigid require-ments imposed by the necessity of building a city which was a microcosm. True, they were the heirs to a long artistic tradition of Hindu origin, to which they were content to conform. But still, in India there are no tem-ples that are pyramid-shaped and topped with five towers. This element so characteristic of Khmer architecture is all the more remarkable because it symbolizes the temple-mountain better than any other known device.

Apparently the desire to embody mythological symbolism in architecture increased rather than diminished toward the end of Khmer civilization. Before the time of Jayavarman VII the ideas of using *naga* balustrades to symbolize the churning, decorating the towers of the temple with the face of the king to proclaim his omnipresence, or reproducing a legendary Himalayan lake in detail by installing hot springs had not been used. To our western taste, these astonishing architectural accomplishments, even when their significance can be comprehended, have something monstrous about them that presage the final decay of an art.

Notwithstanding its symbolism, the great success of Khmer architecture is its appeal to the uninformed as well as to the initiated. At Angkor Wat the knowing visitor realizes he is entering the funeral temple of Suryavarman II under his posthumous title of Paramavishnuloka, 'who has ascended to the supreme world of Vishnu'. He recognizes all the traditional characteristics of a celestial temple, which recalls the form of Meru with its five summits, peopled by innumerable *apsaras*, and decorated with bas-reliefs that evoke the great scenes of the legend of Vishnu and the image of the king who has become consubstantial with a god. The casual visitor who knows nothing of this background is nevertheless full of wonder at the grandeur of the plan, the proportion of the various parts, the mounting levels that seem to rest on one another giving the impression of a pyramid, when truly they are concentric galleries that rise higher and higher. And we conclude by observing that although Khmer architecture

---

11. Banteay Srei lintel, tenth century, picturing the Ramayana story of the rival monkeys, Valin and Surgriva. Minute study of the decorative motifs of the lintels has contributed to establishing the chronology of the Khmer monuments.

is better understood by a comprehension of its symbolism, no explanations are needed to reveal its originality and power.

12. Banteay Srei lintel, tenth century, showing the monster, Ravana, shaking Mount Kailasa. The sacred mountain is interpreted, like Meru in the temple-mountains, as a pyramid with several layers. Siva and his wife, Parvati, are enthroned on top, and below are a row of bearded ascetics, people in animal masks, and animals fleeing in fear.

[VI]

The Mystery of the Bayon

THE Bayon of Angkor Thom is a puzzling monument. It poses problems which archaeologists have answered in varying, and sometimes contradictory, ways. Research has made great progress in recent years, and the time seems to have come to summarize the explanations which are now accepted.

The Bayon has many mysterious features: its complicated plan resulting from successive transformations; the narrow courtyards as deep as wells; the dark galleries; the immense blocks of stone used in its construction which give it a primitive and powerful appearance; the bas-reliefs still partially unexplained; the empty niches; the towers sculptured in the form of faces which are entirely unique in architecture. Everyone who has ever seen the Bayon has been struck by its mysterious quality.

To Doudart de Lagrée[23] the Bayon was 'an architectural wonder of the first order' which 'afforded an amazing sight'. Delaporte[24] saw in it 'a fairy-like construction . . . the most extraordinary of all the Khmer ruins'. Tissandier[25] describes it as 'a structure absolutely unique of its kind', and the architect Fournereau[26] says it is a 'fantastic monument'. Pierre Loti's first impression of the Bayon is memorable: 'I looked up at the tree-covered towers which dwarfed me, when all of a sudden my blood curdled as I saw an enormous smile looking down on me, and then another smile over on another wall, then three, then five, then ten, appearing from every direction. I was being observed from all sides.' But one did not have to be as impressionable as the *pélerin d'Angkor* to react with emotion to the Bayon. Parmentier, the dean of archaeologists in Indochina, whose sensibilities might have been dulled by his daily contact with the monuments, tells us that 'before work started on the Bayon, it was an incomprehensible maze, dangerous to explore, and all the more profoundly affecting and romantic.'

The jungle certainly added a lot of mystery to the Bayon in the condition in which I first saw it in 1912. 'Through thickets of brambles and giant creepers', said Pierre Loti, 'one had to batter out a path to reach this monument. The jungle enlaced it in giant embrace, strangling and crumbling it. Immense fig trees had rooted themselves all over it, growing even from the tops of the towers, reducing them to the function of pedestals. Some of the doorways were completely matted over with a thousand hairy roots.'

The work of Commaille in clearing this garment of green from the Bayon, pulling off the shroud of the forest, has robbed it of much of the romantic appeal that still remains at Ta Prohm. But one must not suppose that the act of uncovering it at the same time laid bare its secrets. On the contrary a clearer view of the monument only revealed a whole series of new problems that had not been evident before. Even after the clearing, the impression of mystery continued to influence the scholars. Fascinated by the enigmatic smiles leering down from the tops of the towers, even the most serious of the archaeologists abandoned their objectivity and gave free play to their imaginations. For instance Marchal, who lived for twenty years in daily contact with the Bayon, wrote the following passage in his *Guide Archéologique aux Temples d'Angkor:*

> This is a confused and bizarre mass, seeming to be a mountain peak that has been shaped and carved by human hands. The impression is both powerful and disconcerting. The complication of the plan of the Bayon makes it all the stranger. It is so impressive that one forgets the faults of its construction, and is entirely preoccupied by its originality. At whatever hour one walks around it, and particularly by moonlight on a clear evening, one feels as if one were visiting a temple in another world, built by an alien people, whose conceptions are entirely unfamiliar. One can imagine one has returned to the fabulous era of legends, when the god Indra built a temple for his son's marriage to the daughter of the king of the Nagas, modelled on his own temple in the celestial world.

The mysteriousness of the Bayon has certainly impeded archaeological research. Perhaps outlining the facts as they are now known will dispel some of the mysteries that have enveloped the Bayon like a fog and will lead to a better understanding of this monument which was at one time the mystic core of the Khmer Empire and the centre of its capital.

We now know that the Bayon is situated at the intersection of the diagonals from the corners of the square walls of Angkor Thom, and thus marks the geometric centre of the city. But this is a fact which was not realized at first. Up to 1908 all the maps of Angkor, beginning with those of the *Voyage d'Exploration* of Doudart de Lagrée and Francis Garnier (1873), and including those of Fournereau (1890) and Tissandier (1893), up to Aymonier (1903), each more or less copied from the ones before, placed the Bayon considerably to the south-east of the centre of the city, which instead was occupied by the Baphuon or the Phimeanakas. The error is understandable, considering the density of the Angkor forest before the work of clearance was begun by the Ecole Française in 1907, the date of the return by Siam of Cambodia's western provinces.

The first topographical maps made by Lieutenants Buat and Ducret of the Service Géographique revealed the correct location of the Bayon. This discovery had important consequences, since once the Bayon was restored to its correct position, it immediately acquired the special importance of a central temple. Its connexion with the four axial gates, executed in the same style and decorated with the same faces, became apparent. The close relationship between the central temple and the four gates was emphasized by two further circumstances revealed by a study of the new map. First, since the Bayon is the only Khmer monument which has no protective wall immediately enclosing it, probably the city wall was substituted for it, and the four gates served as *gopuras*. Second, since the line of the city wall is slightly off centre, an error of two and a half degrees in the western wall, the fact that the central tower of the Bayon rises at the exact intersection of the diagonals of this imperfect square, seems to prove that it was built, at the earliest, at the same time as the walls, and that its position was determined when the ground was still clear by sights drawn from the corners of the walls.

The clearing of the monument by Commaille from 1912 to 1914 revealed that this complicated structure could not have been conceived and executed all at one time. To the penetrating eyes of an architect, the Bayon in its present form is seen to have undergone a series of changes in the course of its construction. This important observation was first made by Parmentier.[27] 'The monument in its present form gives a bizarre impression of accumulation and crowding. The towers rise right next to each other, the structures are too close for easy circulation, and the courts are merely pits without air or light.'

This impression is strongest between the second gallery and the central mass, where there is only enough space for dark passageways, damp and sinister, which as Parmentier said, are certainly a defect in the architecture. Some errors in calculation had been suspected for a long time, or else a change of architectural plan. Parmentier observed:

> The present space between the foundations of the central mass and the pediments over the doors of the lower gallery would not permit the handling of a sculptor's chisel nor certainly allow room for the swinging of his hammer, so that the decoration stones of the terrace have had to remain unfinished, whereas the ornamentation on the opposite side is complete. Moreover the top paving of the terrace in some places forms a ceiling over the passageways below, and the position of these stones has sometimes destroyed the carefully executed sculptures beneath.

In other places, the stones have only walled over the sculptures without destroying them. This is notably the case with the fine pediment representing Lokesvara, the chance discovery of which by Parmentier in 1924, behind and slightly lower than the level of the upper terrace, marked an important date in the history of the studies of the Bayon, and consequently of all Cambodian archaeology.

This is the proof of the first shift in plans. The first plan of the Bayon did not include the enormous structure which we call the central mass. In its place was a group of structures all on the same level, similar to the ones at Ta Prohm and Banteay Kdei.

The observations made by Parmentier at the Bayon in 1924 are not limited to the above conclusions. From various facts, too detailed to repeat here, we can see that sixteen small rooms, each with a passageway at either end, once divided the present court into sixteen small sanctuaries. Inscriptions cut on the uprights of the doors, to the outer gallery tell us that they served as chapels, each containing several statues reproducing the attributes of well-known idols worshipped in the various provincial sanctuaries. Details of the construction prove that these chapels were built after the outer galleries, but before their decoration.

But the architects have detected still other evidence of revisions in the Bayon. Some anomalies in the construction seem to indicate that the four corners of the interior galleries, which are at a slightly lower level than the rest, were not included in the original plan which had the shape of an elaborated cross. Probably the corners which converted the original plan of a cross to a rectangular shape, were added in the course of construction, before the building of the sixteen chapels, since eight of these are supported against the four corner towers, and presuppose their existence.

Additional proof of changes in the plan of the Bayon is that the digging carried on at different times, especially that done by Trouvé in 1935 and by Marchal in 1937, revealed vestiges of a former building whose plan could not be ascertained unless the present building were demolished. At a depth of 3.4 metres underneath the present paving which separates the outer and inner galleries, there is another laterite floor which might have supported a building earlier than the Bayon, because it is only present under the eastern and southern part of the court.

The structure of the interior galleries of the Bayon started from the level of this lower paving. The part of their foundation that has been excavated was found to be panelled for a decoration that was never carried out. At the first period of construction and before two successive fillings lifted the ground level and covered over the foundations, the original cruciform plan had already been changed by adding the four galleries at the corners.

The filling which covered over a foundation whose surface had already been prepared for decoration, lifted the original floor about one metre. It was faced with a laterite paving, indicating that the builders had intended to stop there. But probably it was judged to be too low, because it was later built up 2.4 metres to the present level, at the same time, supposedly, as the building of the outer gallery.

This process of filling is not found only at the Bayon. It is usual in other parts of Angkor Thom, and is especially noticeable at Phimeanakas, whose entire base was lifted more than two metres. It is possible that the raising of the level was due to a flood, a phenomenon often mentioned in Cambodian mythology.[28] We know that the raising of Phimeanakas to a higher level was not prior to the reign of Jayavarman VII (1181 to about 1219) because an inscription of that time was buried in the process. If the lifting of the Bayon was contemporaneous, it must have been done at the latest in the same reign, because

---

13. The Bayon, central temple of Angkor Thom, built by Jayavarman VII, twelfth century. Forty-nine towers carved with gigantic faces on each of four sides, represent the omnipresent power of the god-king.

some of the buildings of the upper layer bear inscriptions attributed to the same king. These buildings, today destroyed, were the sixteen passageway rooms whose foundations only went down as far as the level of the present court.

The architectural history of the Bayon comes to an end with the demolition of these sixteen chapels and the walling up of the passages to the outer gallery which were now useless.

The different changes in the Bayon seem to have taken place in rapid succession. On the one hand the buried foundation of the earliest Bayon was finished with the lack of care that characterized the second half of the twelfth century; it also contains stones re-used from the earlier buildings. On the other hand the inscriptions in the sixteen rooms and the Buddhist decoration cannot have been later than the reign of Jayavarman VII.

Let us now turn to the decoration of this monument, particularly the parts which are unique, that is the bas-reliefs and the faces on the towers.

The bas-reliefs are sculptured on the walls of the outer gallery, and on the rectangular part of the inner gallery. They have been described a number of times by Delaporte,[24] Jules Harmand[29] (1880), and Commaille[30] (1912). The complete photographic record made by Dufour and Carpeaux[31] between 1901 and 1904, and published by the Commission Archéologique de l'Indochine in 1913, has facilitated their study.

---

14. Sculptured towers of the Bayon. 'I looked up at the tree-covered towers which dwarfed me, when all of a sudden my blood curdled as I saw an enormous smile looking down on me, and then another smile on another wall, then three, then five, then ten, appearing in every direction.' *Pierre Loti.*   Photograph by HELEN GARDINER

The bas-reliefs on the outer wall and on the inner gallery differ completely and seem to belong to two different worlds. On the outside is the world of men, of events in history which might actually have taken place, and on the inside is the epic world of gods and legends. Many of the legendary scenes are found repeatedly on Cambodian monuments and can be easily recognized. A number of the historical events pictured by the sculptors have also been identified since the correct dating of the Bayon in the twelfth century directed research to the history of that time.

The faces ornamenting the towers, which are also found on the gates of Angkor Thom, of Ta Prohm, of Banteay Kdei, and of the great Banteay Chmar, are certainly the features which most impress the visitor. Bouillevaux who saw them in 1850, well before Doudart de Lagrée and even before Mouhot, who was incorrectly considered the discoverer of Angkor, called these heads of Buddha 'placid and stupid'. Pierre Loti saw them 'smiling down their flat noses, eyelids half closed, with a kind of decrepit femininity'.

These faces caused the ink to flow in the scholarly world too. The first idea was that they represented Brahma, who was generally sculptured with four faces. This theory was corroborated by local tradition, because they also surmount the gates of Ta Prohm, 'the old Brahma'. This notion was generally accepted until 1902. In that year the *Bulletin de L'Ecole Française d'Extrême-Orient* published Paul Pelliot's translation of the famous account of the Chinese envoy Chou Ta Kuen who visited Angkor in 1296. He informs us that the heads on the gates of the city were five in number, the middle one being covered with gold. Pelliot, commenting on this passage, says,

'One can reconcile this text by interpreting these so-called four-faced Brahmas as five-faced Sivas instead, from which the fifth head on the top has fallen down.'

Louis Finot, continuing with this idea in 1911, recalled that some of the Cham towers, notably Po Nagar at Nha Trang, have as a terminal motif a crowning stone in the form of a *linga*, and also that *lingas* are frequently carved with human faces. He formulated a theory that the towers at the Bayon, with a somewhat phallic form, were enormous *lingas* sculptured with faces, sheltering those worshipped in the shrines inside. This theory was based on the certain belief that the Bayon was a Hindu temple dedicated to Siva. But this theory had to be abandoned when the above-mentioned pediment representing Lokesvara was discovered, a pediment which had formerly been hidden by the central mass. This indicated that the original and basic character of the Bayon was Buddhist. The faces were certainly Buddhist, and probably represented the compassionate Bodhisattva.

Even the archaeologists of the Ecole Française were not able to decide immediately whether the heads on the Bayon were Brahma, Siva, or Buddha. The distinctions which, for instance, clearly differentiate the Olympian gods are not so marked in Indian religions; Brahma is the Creator of the Universe; Siva spreads blessings on every region in space; Buddha of the Great Miracle duplicates himself in infinity; and Lokesvara faces in all directions. The spirit behind these Indian divinities, which the architect tried to represent, was not so much a real being, an individual, but an abstraction. Pierre Loti grasped this with the remarkable perception of a poet, and expressed it in a striking way: 'From on high the four faces on each of these towers face the four cardinal points, looking out in every direction from beneath lowered eyelids. Each face has the same ironic expression of pity, the same smile. They proclaim and repeat in a haunting way the omnipresence of the god of Angkor.' We know that this god of Angkor was the king, the god-king, personified before the twelfth century by a golden *linga*, and at the time of the Bayon by the statue of Buddha, which was recovered from the bottom of an open pit under the central tower. The work of Paul Mus completely confirmed the intuitive observation of Loti, proving that the abstract conception intended by the sculptors of the Bayon was 'the royal power blessing the four quarters of the country'. Brahma, Siva, or Lokesvara would serve equally well to express the abstract idea, and though we have settled on Lokesvara, we have done so because of the clearly Buddhist character of the other parts of the Bayon.

We now come to the question of what cult was practised inside the sanctuary. The pediment of Lokesvara proves that the original Bayon was not a temple with a *linga*, as had been thought before, but a Buddhist sanctuary dedicated to Lokesvara. This fact was again confirmed in 1933 by the discovery of the original idol in the central sanctuary, the enormous statue of Buddha which His Majesty King Monivong took to give to the cult of his subjects in 1935, and which was installed in a pavilion south of the avenue leading from the Royal Palace to the Gate of Victory.

In 1934 I conceived the idea that this statue, like the other idols in the Bayon, was an image of apotheosis representing King Jayavarman VII in the form of Buddha, and taking the same place in Buddhism as did the god-king in the Sivaite worship.

The multiplication of these faces to the four cardinal points symbolizes the idea that the royal power is blessing the four quarters of the kingdom. As for the repetition of these faces on every tower, Paul Mus has an ingenious explanation. The idols worshipped in the chapels inside the towers were statues of deified princes or dignitaries, or else of local gods.

> Perhaps each tower corresponded to a province of the kingdom, or at least to a religious or administrative centre of the province. Thus if the four faces symbolized the royal power spreading over the land in every direction, placing them over the chapel which was typical of each province signified that Jayavarman VII's royal power was as strong in the provinces as at Angkor itself. This accounted for having a four-faced tower to represent each part of the kingdom. We now begin to understand this mysterious architecture as the symbol of the Great Miracle of Jayavarman VII. It represents his administrative and religious power extending to every corner of Cambodian territory by means of this unique sign.

The Bayon is constructed on top of an earlier monument. There is no proof that the first structure, although built near the centre of the city, was originally supposed to be the central temple. The Baphuon, which was at the centre of an enclosure not so very different from Angkor Thom, had fulfilled this role ever since the middle of the ninth century. The builder of the first Bayon, whether it was Jayavarman at the very beginning of his reign, or whether it was one of his immediate predecessors, might only have intended to build an additional temple in the capital, and to create not a temple-mountain, but a Buddhist sanctuary all on one level, similar to Ta Prohm or Banteay Kdei.

After Jayavarman VII had repulsed the Chams, who

had sacked Angkor in 1177, and after he had been crowned in 1181, he conceived of the ambitious scheme of restoring the capital and completely surrounding it for the first time with a solid wall of rock. He was necessarily obliged by age-long tradition to erect a temple-mountain.

It is more than likely that Jayavarman made use of the foundation of the Bayon, which either had been started under his predecessors or more probably at the very beginning of his own reign, to transform it into a temple-mountain, for the purpose of enshrining his own statue in the form of Buddha-king. To do this he had to modify the existing incomplete construction. In order to make room for the enormous central tower and the chapels encircling it, the central mass had to be constructed directly against the interior gallery.

Moreover it is noteworthy that the addition of the four corners of the interior gallery, obscuring its original shape, corresponds on a much larger scale to the masking over of the base of the central tower of the Baphuon. I do not think it is too far-fetched to suppose that this emphasized the idea of cosmic mountain which the builders wished to convey.

Thus in my opinion the construction of the central mass and the addition of the four corners to the inner gallery were both attributable to the same idea, the transformation of the original Bayon into a royal temple.

The adaption of the former Sivaite cult to the god-king of Buddhism probably did not survive the life of the ruler who began it. We know from various sources that the Buddhist fervour which impregnated the aristocracy during his reign was followed by a violent Brahman reaction. There were acts of vandalism of which the Bayon and other Buddhist monuments bear violent traces.

At this period, the middle of the thirteenth century, the removal of the sixteen chapels probably took place, as well as the destruction of the Great Buddha, found broken to pieces in the pit underneath. The Buddhist idols were beheaded and replaced by *lingas* and other Sivaite symbols. These were in turn destroyed by a new form of Buddhism which was introduced from Ceylon through Burma and Siam and established permanently in the country which it still dominates.

[VII]

Jayavarman II, Founder of the Royal Dynasty of Angkor

UNTIL recently Jayavarman II was known only as the king who established the Cambodian dynasty in the region of Angkor in the ninth century. Not one monument could be definitely attributed to him. His true importance began to be recognized after the mission of Stern and de Coral-Rémusat in 1936.[32]

The work of that mission, inspired by the earlier research of Parmentier, Goloubew, and Marchal, and followed by the studies of Dupont in 1937,[33] identified some important temples and statues as the connecting links between pre-Angkorian and Angkorian art in Cambodia. This chain of research has been one of the most outstanding accomplishments of the archaeologists in Cambodia in recent years.

Its effectiveness was due to a collaboration between epigraphy and the history of art. Epigraphy furnished the historical background and a few reliable dates as guideposts. The minute study of the evolution of artistic forms established a relative chronology of the monuments, which the epigraphic evidence corroborated.

As we have said, Jayavarman II was the first ruler to establish the seat of the Cambodian monarchy in the

---

15. Good spirits supporting a *naga* balustrade leading over the moat to one of the five towered entrances to Angkor Thom. Evil spirits with bulging eyes and grimacing mouths hold the *naga* on the opposite side.
Photograph by HELEN GARDINER

region of Angkor. We know that during the two previous
centuries the kings of Kambuja, after freeing themselves
from the yoke of Funan in the middle of the sixth century, and after little by little ejecting their former sovereign from the valley of the Mekong, established the
centre of their power in what is now the southern and
eastern part of Cambodia. The greater part of the pre-
Angkorian monuments and of the inscriptions of the sixth
and seventh centuries are found in that region. We must
not suppose, however, that the western region around the
Grand Lac was not also under their control. In the environs of Siem Reap and Battambang and even west of
the frontier of 1907 there are a few pre-Angkorian sanctuaries with inscriptions, citing the names of King Isanavarman and Jayavarman I. However, these monuments are comparatively isolated and unimportant.
During the sixth and seventh centuries the heart of the
kingdom was in the lower Mekong valley.

At the beginning of the eighth century Chinese records
report that Cambodia was divided into two parts, Cambodia of the sea to the south, 'bounded by the ocean
and covered with lakes', and to the north, Cambodia
of the land, 'filled with mountains and valleys'. For a
long time scholars supposed that these two parts corresponded to the region of present-day Cambodia, and that
Cambodia of the sea had its centre at Angkor Borei, and
Cambodia of the land had its capital at Sambor on the
Mekong.

Epigraphic research enabled me to correct these mis-

16.   Bas-relief from the Bayon, showing carved wooden construction of
human habitations, with tile roofs. The stone temples were purely religious
buildings. Even the palaces of the kings were built of wood, no vestige of
which remains today.

takes, which had originated at the very beginning of Cambodian studies. I showed in an article in the *Bulletin de l'Ecole Française* in 1936 that actually Cambodia of the land corresponded to lower and middle Laos. Cambodia of the sea included the entire basin of the Mekong, where, during the eighth century, there was constant shifting of peoples and power. Inscriptions prove that numerous dynasties with changing capitals existed there. The two most important were Sambor on the Mekong, and Aninditapura, whose location has long been sought in vain. A union between these two principalities was brought about by a prince of Aninditapura, to whom, later, Jayavarman II claimed to be related.

The history of the eighth century is very obscure. One fact is clear. The disturbances which troubled the region were connected with events in the Malayan archipelago. The eighth century was a period of ferment in these southern waters during which new empires rose and new dynasties were formed. In south-east Sumatra the Malayan kingdom of Srivijaya had emerged at the end of the seventh century, and in the beginning of the eighth century it began to spread its dominion over the peninsula, establishing the beginning of its hold over the straits of this island kingdom.[34] In Java another new kingdom resurrected the imperial title, 'King of the Mountain', formerly used by the rulers of Funan, indicating its pretension to dominion over the universe.

The expansion of the Malayan kingdom of Sumatra and the ascension of an ambitious dynasty in Java had their repercussions on the coast of Indochina, where we have numerous evidences of maritime raids from the south.

In 767 these invaders, who had penetrated as far as

Son Tay, in Tonkin, were defeated and pushed into the sea by the Chinese governor, Tchang Po Yi, the founder of the city of Dai La-thanh, the ancient site of Hanoi. In 774 the Javanese ravaged the coast of South Annam where we find Cham inscriptions, notably the one at Po Nagar in Nha Trang, describing these 'man-eaters' with horror. These men, 'born in foreign lands, living on a diet even more horrible than human corpses, frightening, very black and thin, terrible and dangerous as death, who came in boats', pillaged the temple of the goddess. In 787 another inscription describes a new raid in the same region by the 'armies of Java who landed in boats'.

We have still another account of the Javanese sorties in Cambodia from an Arabian source, written one hundred and fifty years after the event. In 916 Abu Zayd wrote down the account of a trader, Sulayman. Here is a résumé of the tale from the translation of Gabriel Ferrand.[35]

A Khmer king, 'young and hot-headed', was talking one day with his minister about the Maharajah, the Emperor of the Southern Seas. 'I have a wish', said the king. 'I would like to behold the head of the Maharajah before me on a platter.' And notwithstanding the warnings of his minister, he kept repeating his wish, until it passed from mouth to mouth, and finally reached the ears of the Maharajah himself. The Maharajah declared that this foolhardy young ruler deserved a good lesson, and pretending to start off on a voyage of inspection of his kingdom, he set sail directly for Cambodia. He had no trouble in sailing up the river to the capital, entering the palace and seizing the king. 'You have expressed a desire to see my head before you on a platter', he said. 'If you had also said that you wished to seize my country, I would have done the same to yours. But as you only ex-

pressed the first of these desires, I will be content to give
you the treatment you wished to try on me, and to return
to my country without molesting yours.' Then he had
the prince beheaded, and ordered the prime minister to
proclaim a new king. Then the Maharajah departed immediately to return to his country without taking a single thing, or allowing any of his followers to do so. When
he arrived back in his kingdom, he seated himself on a
throne which overlooked a lake, and he had the platter
containing the king's head placed before him. Then he
summoned all his ministers and related what had happened. After that he had the head washed and embalmed
and placed in a jar, and sent it to the successor of the
former king along with a letter explaining that this
had been a personal revenge only, and that he drew
no glory from his victory. 'When the news of these events
reached the kings of India and China, the Maharajah
rose in their estimation. From that time on the kings of
the land of the Khmers turned their faces in the direction of the Maharajah's country every morning and bow-
ed down to the ground in homage to him.'

It appears from this account that following the expedition, the Maharajah, that is the Emperor of the
Southern Seas, exercised more or less effective control
over the Khmer Empire in the eighth century. This fact
is also confirmed by epigraphic texts, from which I will
try to reconstruct some of the reign of Jayavarman II.

He was related to the former Cambodian dynasty in
a tenuous manner. He is generally referred to as the
great grand-nephew through the female line of a prince
of Aninditapura, who annexed the kingdom of Sambor.
An inscription from the beginning of the tenth century,
speaking of his accession, says, 'For the prosperity of the

people, from this perfectly pure race of kings, like a great lotus which no longer bears its stem, he sprang up in fresh bloom.' The official genealogists often used this kind of veiled metaphor in order to avoid the upheavals attendant on any change in the dynastic line.

Jayavarman II left no inscription of his own, a unique circumstance in Cambodian history. At least to this date, none has ever been found. Luckily the main events of his reign have been recorded with quite a wealth of detail in the fine stele of the eleventh century which came from the region of Aranya and which is preserved in the Bangkok Museum. It is the famous stele of Sdok Kak Thom, from which an incorrectly interpreted passage misled scholars for a long time to a false chronology. As a result they believed that the first Angkor of the ninth century was centred in the Bayon, whereas its central temple was really the Bakheng. To reconstruct the biography of Jayavarman II we have only to follow this stele, which was translated by Louis Finot in 1915 in the *Bulletin de l'Ecole Française*.

'His Majesty', says the text, 'came from Java to reign in the city of Indrapura.' Although the name Java in some ancient texts refers not only to the island of Java, but also to Sumatra and to Malaya, in this case we have reason to think it really referred to Java. The family of Jayavarman II which, as we have seen, was distantly connected with a Cambodian dynasty of the eighth century, probably fled to the southern island at the time of the disturbances or else was forced to retreat there during one of the wartime raids referred to above.

His return from Java took place around 800, because we have several proofs of the fact that his formal reign began about 802. The country was probably in a condition of total anarchy without any ruler, and the young prince had to reconquer the kingdom before he could exert his rights or lay claim to the Cambodian throne.

He first established himself in the city of Indrapura. Several indications guided me in locating a city of that name in the province of Thbong Khmum, east of Kompong Cham.[4] The capital of Jayavarman II may have been either at Banteay Prei Nokor, whose name seems to indicate it was once a capital, and whose pre-Angkorian monuments are in the style of the ninth century, or else at the site of some ruins in Baray Occidental, which will be discussed later.

Apparently at Indrapura the king took a Brahman scholar, Sivakaivalya, as his chaplain, a man who was to follow him in all his moves, and who was to become the first officiating priest of a new cult, the cult of the god-king.

After staying for a time in Indrapura, Jayavarman II left his residence, accompanied by his chaplain and his chaplain's family, and moved to the north of the Grand Lac, in the region where the first city of Angkor was to be built a century later. 'When they arrived at the eastern district', says the stele, 'the king granted some land and also the village called Kuti to the family of his chaplain.' Since this stele was written in the middle of the eleventh century, at a time when Angkor had already occupied its present situation for a century and a half, the 'eastern district' referred to must be a region east of present-day Angkor. The name of Kuti has survived in that of Banteay Kdei, a much later monument, but with an earlier site adjacent to it. In 1930 Marchal discovered a group of three towers a little north of Banteay Kdei,

which I had hoped to identify with Kuti or Kutisvara
of the ninth century. In its present form the monument
does not antedate the tenth century, but it seems that
one part of the central tower may be older.[36] 'Then',
continues the stele, 'the king reigned in the city of Hariharalaya. The chaplain too established himself in that
city, and the members of his family were appointed in the
corps of pages.'

With Hariharalaya we are beginning to deal with a
more identifiable region and one more abundant in monuments. In 1928 I suggested identifying this ancient capital with the Roluos group, situated fifteen kilometres
south-east of Siem Reap. This group includes the temples
of Bakong, Prah Ko, and Lolei. This last name is probably a faint echo of the old name Hariharalaya. In 1936
an inscription was discovered which proved my assump-
tion correct. However, Bakong, Prah Ko, and Lolei are
more recent than the reign of Jayavarman II, and go
back only to the end of the eleventh century.

At Indrapura and at Hariharalaya, Jayavarman II had
installed himself in old cities or at least in cities that had
been built before he moved into them. But now he began
his work as a builder. 'After this', reads the stele, 'the
king founded the city of Amarendrapura, and the royal
chaplain went to live there too in order to serve the king.'
In 1924, that is to say at a time when the style of the
Bayon was still thought to belong to the ninth century,
Georges Groslier took up the former hypothesis of Aymonier, attempting to identify Amarendrapura with the
great temple of Banteay Chmar. But we know now that
this monument is no earlier than the twelfth century.
Groslier's reasons for thinking that Amarendrapura was
situated in north-western Cambodia were partly justifi-

ed. But that region contains no monuments which according to their architecture and decoration could have belonged to the reign of Jayavarman II. Also one cannot figure out why, having once installed himself at Angkor, he should have chosen a region so far from the Grand Lac, and one that must always have been barren. On the other hand aerial research by Goloubew, Lagisquet, and Commander Terrasson on the area near the edge of the western containing wall of Baray Occidental has revealed a series of enclosures around ruined buildings, which, judging by their style, must date from the first period of Angkorian art. One of them, Prasat Ak Yom, discovered by Trouvé in 1932 shows many repetitions of pre-Angkorian style.[37] Could this group possibly be the city of Amarendrapura founded by Jayavarman II? Let us hope that some day a new epigraphic discovery will help us decide. At present this theory is in question because the style of some of the ruins seems to be earlier than the time of Jayavarman II.

Now we come to the high point in the reign. After having founded Amarendrapura, the king left his new capital and established himself at Mahendraparvata, that is at Phnom Kulen, the sandstone hill which dominates the plain of Angkor with its wooded peak, and whose blue silhouette rises on the northern horizon.

'Then', says the inscription, 'His Majesty went to rule at Mahendraparvata. The chaplain also went and installed himself there in order to serve the king as before. Then a Brahman scholar, well versed in magic, came from Janapada at the invitation of the king to establish a ritual, in order that Cambodia might no longer be

17. Khrishna Govardhana, Angkor Borei, sixth century, National Museum, Phnom Penh, showing the freedom and grace of pre-Khmer sculpture.

dependent on Java, and that there might be only one king ruling the country. This Brahman recited the texts from beginning to end, to teach them to the chaplain, and he instructed him how to institute the ritual of the god-king.'

In the preceding chapters the cult of the god-king has frequently been discussed. Here I will simply repeat that the 'essence of royalty' or, as it is called in certain texts, 'the essence of self' of the king was supposed to reside in a *linga*, the symbol of the creative power of Siva, ensconced in a pyramid at the centre of the royal city which, in turn, was situated at the axis of the world. This miraculous *linga*, a sort of palladium of the kingdom, was generally considered to have been obtained from Siva with the help of a Brahman who presented it to the original king of the dynasty. The communion between the king and the god took place on a sacred mountain, whether natural or artificial. This legend is akin to ancient Mesopotamian beliefs. Many Indian dynasties also had their sacred mountains. The kings of Funan had their hill at Ba Phnom. As I mentioned above, the kings who ruled in Java in the eighth century belonged to the dynasty of the Sailendra, in other words, of the Kings of the Mountain. Jayavarman II, in order to free himself of the dominion of the Kings of the Mountain, who, as their title implied, considered themselves rulers of the universe, had to become one himself. He had to receive on a mountain top, from a Brahman, the miraculous *linga* in which the imperial power of the Khmer kings would reside from that time on. That is why he moved to Phnòm Kulen

18. Feminine divinity, Koh Krieng, eighth century, National Museum, Phnom Penh. This figure is completely frontal, and solid, but still supple in its feeling.

and sent for a Brahman from Janapada who instituted
the cult of the god-king and taught it to the king's chaplain.

One may well ask why Jayavarman did not under-
take this rite at the beginning of his reign, and why
he waited to live in three different capitals before he
proclaimed his independence. Maybe it was because he
first had to conquer and pacify the various parts of his
realm and thus unify it before he could turn his attention to installing the miraculous *linga*, the symbol of his
power. Perhaps these moves from one capital to another
were accompanied by military campaigns about which
we have no record. An inscription of the eleventh century simply says that the 'king ordered his principal offi-
cers to pacify every district.'

In the following centuries Jayavarman's installation
at Phnom Kulen was thought of as an historic event
which marked the beginning of a new era. The inscriptions constantly refer to Jayavarman II as the king who
established his residence at the summit of Mount Mahendra. But is there anything left of his palaces there?

The buildings scattered on top of the plateau of
Phnom Kulen were completely engulfed in the forest, and
were only discovered little by little. Fifty years ago so
little was known of them that writers like Aymonier and
Louis Finot thought the expression 'residence on Mount
Mahendra' was only a metaphor, and they searched for
this city, not at the top, but around the foot of the hill.
They suggested Beng Mealea or Prah Khan at Angkor,
but the chronology established later eliminated them
from consideration. Further research on Phnom Kulen
led to the discovery of a number of additional monuments. They revealed a style which formed a link be-

tween pre-Angkorian art and the art of the early Angkorian period, which can be considered as dating from
the reign of Jayavarman II.[38] They are probably the
vestiges of the capital he founded there.

We do not know how long the capital remained at
Kulen. 'After that', the inscription tells us, 'the king went
back to rule at Hariharalaya, and the god-king was
brought there too. The chaplain and all his relations continued to officiate as before. The chaplain died during
that reign. The king died in the city of Hariharalaya,
where the god-king resided. The god-king resided in every
capital where the king took him, and acted as the protector of the royal power of the successive rulers.'

Thus we see that Jayavarman II, after his stay at
Kulen, returned for a second time to Hariharalaya
where he died in 850 after a reign of forty-eight years.

Although we know that Jayavarman's capital at
Hariharalaya can be identified with the Roluos group,
we cannot definitely decide on the location of the royal
city. The question is complicated by the fact that Jayavarman II made two stays at Hariharalaya, separated
by the time at Kulen, and also because that city remained the capital for forty years after his death, up to
the reign of Yasovarman, the founder of the first Angkor.
I have already eliminated the three principal monuments
of the group. Lolei dates from 893, Prah Ko from 879,
and Bakong from 881. The buildings which according to
their style might be earlier have all undergone some re-
building, perhaps by Jayavarman II himself, or by his
successors. The most characteristic and the most important is Trapeang Phong, whose two styles, revealed by
the excavations of Lagisquet in 1936, may date from the
two stays of Jayavarman II at Hariharalaya.

Guided by the research of Philippe Stern, Mme. de Coral-Rémusat, and Dupont, we must try to distinguish the special characteristics of the buildings of Jayavarman II in the evolution of Khmer art.

Beginning in 1932 Philippe Stern made a detailed study of the several sculptures from Phnom Kulen which enabled him to piece together a distinct style for the period of Jayavarman II which formed a transition between the pre-Angkorian and Angkorian styles.[39] In identifying the few buildings that had been discovered on Phnom Kulen at that time as belonging to the reign of Jayavarman II, he was only reviewing and clarifying a theory already formulated by Parmentier in his *Art Khmer Primitif* and by himself in his book on the Bayon, in which he confirmed and enlarged his former thesis.

He relied less on the architecture, which was quite restrained, than on decoration and statuary to work out the evolution of Khmer art and thus to establish a chronology of the monuments. The decoration of the brick towers, all that need be considered now, was limited to the stone setting of the door, that is, the two columns on either side and the lintel. The study of these elements can be followed step by step from pre-Angkorian time to their culmination in the Angkorian epoch.

In pre-Angkorian art the columns are round. The principal motif on the lintel is bow-shaped, ornamented with medallions and scrolls, and its outer ends rest on the consoles forming the upper ends of the columns or sometimes emerge from the jaws of *makaras* that face inward.

In the Angkor period the columns are octagonal. The bow shape on the lintel becomes a branch, either straight or curving, whose ends either unroll outwards or terminate in *makaras* that face outward. The curving

lines take the form of leaves or other foliate motifs, and
there is a central medallion in the form of a rose, a ped-
estal, or an animal head.

If we examine the settings of the doors at Phnom
Kulen, we find that some of the columns are octagonal
as at Angkor, and some of them square, forming a
transition between the round and the octagonal. Their
decoration is more restrained than at Angkor, and is
made up of a little leaf, seen from the front, repeated
at regular intervals and without any intermediary decoration.

The lintels of Kulen show great diversity. Some have
older motifs, bow-shaped with medallions, garlands and
scrolls, *makaras* facing inward Others have newer features, that is, the bow shape is in the form of branches
with a leaf decoration and has a central motif in the form
of an animal head, or *makaras* facing outward.

This decoration of the door settings indicates that the
art of the time of Jayavarman II was in a transitional
period. The statuary gives the same indication.

'Briefly', Stern wrote, 'the columns prove the unity
of style, and the lintels indicate how extraordinarily
fertile and varied the art of the epoch was. Inspiration
was sought on every side, and borrowed motifs were
mixed and re-created. The statues corroborate the architectural decoration of Kulen and show as much relation
to the past as they indicate the direction of the style to
come.'

Of the foreign influences which left their impression
on the style of the time of Jayavarman II and gave it
a special flavour, two were particularly important, those
of Java and Champa.

A certain measure of Javanese influence should not

come as a surprise considering Jayavarman II's origin.
Goloubew first pointed this out in 1930. Mme. de Coral-
Rémusat enumerated the following features as inspired
by Javanese influence: the decoration of the pilasters
with a continuous scroll design, the substitution of *dvar-
apalas* and *apsaras* for the image of a palace found in
pre-Angkorian art, the costumes and jewelry, and the
type of *garuda* ornamenting the lintels.

As for the Cham influence, it cannot be explained
historically, but it is impossible to deny. It is evident
mostly in details of ground plan and of architecture.
Philippe Stern says that Prasat Damrei Krap gives the
impression of being a sanctuary built by a Cham architect, with elements of Khmer decoration added, particularly the sandstone doors indisputably sculptured by
Khmer artists in the Khmer tradition.

Such is the art of Jayavarman II, a traditional style,
which was unrecognized a few years ago and which
fortunately fills in a missing link in the evolution of
Khmer art.

This long reign of forty-eight years left an indelible
mark on the country. Jayavarman II, while unifying
and pacifying his kingdom, seemed to be seeking out the
future location of the capital, near enough to the supply
of fish in the Grand Lac but beyond the reach of the
annual floods, convenient to the sandstone quarry of
Phnom Kulen, and sufficiently close to the passes giving
access to the plateau of Korat and the valley of the Menam. Like a bird of prey soaring over the land, he moved from Hariharalaya to Amarendrapura to Phnom
Kulen, pivoting in a circle around the future Angkor,
where his great nephew and third successor was to
found the city of Yasodharapura, destined to remain

the site of the Khmer capital for six hundred years.

Jayavarman II instituted the cult of the god-king, who as the stele at Sdok Kak Thom says, 'resided in each capital to which the king took him, serving as a protector of the royal power for the successive rulers.' The god-king's sanctuary in the form of a pyramid built on a mountain, either natural or artificial, marked the centre of the royal city from that time on.

We know all this from the inscriptions after the reign of Jayavarman II and through recent discoveries of epigraphic sources, which fully corroborate them. Jayavarman II, unlike some of his very loquacious successors, left not a single text. Perhaps he was too busy with the present to have time for posterity, and like all truly great men, he combined authority with modesty. A Sanskrit poem in his praise by a court poet half a century after his death says, 'He seated himself on the heads of lions that ornamented his throne, he imposed his will on the heads of kings, he established his residence on the head of Mount Mahendra, and still there was no pride in him.'

The Last Great King of Angkor,
Jayavarman VII

THE true history of Jayavarman VII which has been
revealed by scholars in this century has gradually
restored to the Cambodians a feeling of pride in
being the descendants of the ancient Khmers.

This king was completely ignored by any annals or
local records and was entirely forgotten by the Cambodians. He was considered a king of secondary importance by the historians, and the rapid decay of the
country was supposed to have begun under his reign.
Jayavarman VII's reputation did not begin to grow until
1903 when Louis Finot published a Sanskrit inscription
in the *Bulletin de l'Ecole Française*, which had been discovered by Georges Maspero at Say Fong close to Vientiane,
and which recorded the founding of a hospital in 1186.
Finot noticed that the text was identical with one on a
stele found on the gulf of Siam, near the frontier of Cochin China, and he also remembered that Jayavarman
VII was often mentioned in Cham inscriptions as a great
conqueror. He concluded, 'At present these steles, which
re-echo each other from the interior of Laos to the coasts
of Annam and lower Cochin China, attest to his victo-
ries and his acts of mercy, and indicate that this hereto-

---

19. Siva between his two wives, Uma and Ganga, from Bakong, ninth
century. This triple statue gives the effect of being carved from a single
block of stone. Its simplicity is typical of early Khmer sculpture.

fore obscure figure of the Cambodian past must have been a great prince.'

The obscurity surrounding him has certainly been cleared away during the last fifty years of patient research, and the opinion of Louis Finot has been fully confirmed. This king, of whom nothing more than his name was known in 1900 when the Ecole Française d'Extrême-Orient was created, is now considered one of the greatest rulers of Cambodia. He extended his country to its furthest limits annexing for a time the kingdom of Champa, and covered his capital and his provinces with a prodigious number of monuments.

The numerous inscriptions Jayavarman VII left are the sources used to support this biography of him. There are the well-known inscriptions at Ta Prohm, Prah Khan, and Banteay Chmar, all three of which were published in the *Bulletin de l'Ecole Française d'Extrême-Orient*. Then there are the edicts on the hospitals, the large stele found in 1916 at the foot of the pyramid of Phimeanakas in the Royal Palace at Angkor Thom, and a Cham inscription at Mi-son translated by Louis Finot and also published in the *Bulletin de l'Ecole*.

Jayavarman VII's genealogy is known exactly. Through his father, who had a short reign around 1155, he was a cousin of the conquering King Suryavarman II, who had led his armies as far as Tonkin, and whose funeral temple is Angkor Wat. Through his mother he was descended from the royal dynasty of foreign origin which ruled Cambodia throughout the eleventh century

---

20. Elephant from Mebon Oriental, second half of the tenth century. All four corners of each layer of this pyramid are guarded by life-size elephants, typical of the Khmer talent for using architectural sculpture.

and which was related through a female line to the
pre-Angkorian kings of Cambodia.

Jayavarman was born around 1120, or at the latest
in 1125, during the reign of Suryavarman II, and he
married, probably at a very young age, the princess
Jayarajadevi who was to exert a great influence over him.

At an unknown date the prince Jayavarman left Cambodia to conduct an expedition against Champa, at
Vijaya, that is the present Binh-dinh. For the princess
the absence of her husband seems to have been a source
of great chagrin, which is described in an inscription in
the Royal Palace written by her sister. The text describes
the wife bathed in tears, weeping like Sita for her departed husband, offering prayers for his return, turning
in her sorrow to the ascetic practices of Brahmanism, and
finally finding comfort in Buddhism.

'Taught by her older sister, Indradevi', says the stele,
'considering Buddha as the well-loved object of her aspi-
rations, she followed in the serene path of the sage, who
walked between the fire of torments and the sea of sor-
rows.'

During Jayavarman's stay at Champa, his father King
Dharanindravarman II died. His successor was Yasovarman, the second of that name, whose parentage is unknown. The reign of Yasovarman was remembered for a
dramatic incident recorded in the temple of Banteay
Chmar, and illustrated on a bas-relief on the same monument. King Yasovarman was attacked by a mysterious
being, whom the text calls Rahu and whom the relief also
pictures as Rahu. This was the mythological monster
who was supposed to devour the sun and the moon when
an eclipse occurred. The King was rescued by a young
prince who was probably the son of Jayavarman. The

colourful inscription relating this incident has already been quoted in Chapter III.

Soon after, in 1165, Yasovarman II fell victim to another dignitary, who proclaimed himself king under the name of Tribhuvanaditya, 'the sun of three worlds'. When this news reached Champa, the stele tells us, Jayavarman 'hastened back to come to the aid of King Yasovarman'. Probably he also wanted to make good his own right to the succession. 'But since Yasovarman had already been despoiled of his kingdom and his life by the usurper, Jayavarman remained at home in Cambodia to rescue the land which was weighed down with crimes, waiting for a propitious moment. The princess, having regained her husband by her exertions, stopped her prayers. She wanted him to rescue the land from the ocean of misfortune in which it had been plunged.'

In other words, Jayavarman who had arrived too late and who found the usurper installed on his throne, did not leave again for Champa, but at the instigation of his wife, stayed in Cambodia, 'waiting for the propitious moment'. He was destined to wait fifteen years.

About 1166, at the same time that a rebel took possession of the Cambodian throne, an adventurer by the name of Jaya Indravarman seized the throne of Champa. One of his first moves was to conciliate Annam, or at least to assure himself of its friendly neutrality. In 1170 he sent an ambassador carrying gifts to Emperor Li Anh Ton. Then, sure of his northern frontier, he turned his attention to Cambodia.

' Jaya Indravarman, king of the Chams, as audacious as the demon Ravana, transported his army on chariots and set out to attack the land of Kambu, similar to the sky', says the stele found in the Royal Palace.

But the battle was indecisive. Then Jaya Indravarman changed his plan and decided to surprise Cambodia from the sea. The expedition took place in 1177. Following the coast, the Cham navy, piloted by a shipwrecked Chinese, arrived at the mouth of the Mekong and sailed up to the Grand Lac. Angkor was taken by surprise, and the usurper Tribhuvanaditya was killed. The Cham army pillaged the city and collected an enormous amount of booty.

The throne was left vacant. Jayavarman figured that his time had come, but before proclaiming himself king, he had to rid the country of the invaders. He fought a series of battles against the Chams, notably a naval battle which is pictured on the walls of the Bayon and of Banteay Chmar in almost identical fashion. These battles finally liberated the country.

In 1181, four years after the invasion, Cambodia had been restored to calm, and Jayavarman had himself crowned king at the same time that he undertook the restoration of the capital. 'The city of Yasodharapura, like a young maiden of good family well matched with her fiancé and burning with desire, decorated with a palace of precious stones and clothed in its ramparts, was married by the king for the procreation of good fortune for his people, celebrated by a magnificent feast under the dais where his glory was displayed.' This is the way one of the steles placed at the corner of the wall of Angkor Thom describes the ceremony. This city which the king is supposed to have married was the city of Angkor Thom, not that of the ninth century centred in the temple of Phnom Bakheng, but the present city with the Bayon at its centre.

From the time of the Cham invasion of 1177 Jayavarman had sworn, says the Chinese historian, Ma Tuan Lin[40], 'to be completely revenged on his enemies, an oath he was finally able to fulfil after eighteen years of patient dissimulation'.

But before keeping his oath and carrying the war to the kingdom of the Chams he had to deal with a revolt in his own states which broke out at Malyang, in the southern part of Battambang. To put it down he called on the assistance of a young Cham prince who was a refugee. A Cham inscription from Mi-son carries this account:

> Prince Vidyanandana went to Cambodia in 1182 in the prime of his youth. The king of Cambodia (that is Jayavarman VII who had ascended the throne the previous year) seeing that he carried the thirty-three marks of a predestined man, took him to his heart and taught him all the princely sciences and feats of arms. At the time he lived in Cambodia there was a village in that kingdom called Malyang, populated by a group of bad men who revolted against the king. The king seeing that this prince was very accomplished in the arts of war, gave him the responsibility of leading the Cambodian troops to capture the city of Malyang. He carried out everything according to the wish of the king of Cambodia. The king seeing his worth, conferred on him the title of Yuvaraja and gave him all the benefits and all the rewards which Cambodia could offer.

The young Cham prince also helped Jayavarman to take revenge against Champa. This revenge, the fruit of long years of 'patient dissimulation', to quote the Chinese historian again, had been prepared for by securing the neutrality of Emperor Li Cao Ton of Annam. Then he had only to wait for the propitious moment. This presented itself in 1190 on the occasion of a new attack by his old enemy Jaya Indravarman IV.

We do not know if he himself took part in the campaign against Champa. An inscription in the temple of
Po Nagar in Nha Trang says that he 'conquered the capital of Champa and carried off all the *lingas*'. In any
case he entrusted the leadership of his troops to Vidyanandana, who seized the capital, Vijaya (Binh-Dinh), and
the king, Jaya Indravarman, whom he sent back to Cambodia as a prisoner. In his place, Vidyanandana installed
a young Cambodian prince, the brother-in-law of Jayavarman VII. For himself he carved out a kingdom to
the south in the region of Panduranga, that is Phan-rang.
Thus Champa was divided between two kings, one related to the Cambodian king, and the other his vassal. This
state of things did not last long. By means of a revolt at
Binh-Dinh which chased away the brother-in-law of Jayavarman VII, Vidyanandana shook off the yoke of the
king of Cambodia and re-unified the country to his own
advantage, after having killed the former king, Jaya Indravarman IV, whom Jayavarman VII had released
from prison to fight against him. Not until 1203 was
Vidyanandana finally driven out by one of his uncles
who had been bribed by the Cambodians. From 1203 to
1220 Champa was truly a province of Cambodia.

Jayavarman VII's difficulties with his neighbours on
the east did not, however, prevent him from extending
his kingdom to the north and west. The Cambodian
inscription found the furthest north—the one already
mentioned from Say Fong next to Vientiane—dates
from his reign. Chinese historians record that he also
subjugated part of the Malay Peninsula and pushed his
conquests into Burma. One of his inscriptions, the one
from Prah Khan, informs us that the water for the ritual
ablution was furnished by Suryabhatta and the other

Brahmans, the king of Java (the king of the Yavanas), and the two kings of Champa. Suryabhatta was probably the chief Brahman at the court. The king of the Yavanas was the emperor of Annam, Long Can, son of Li Anh Ton, who ascended to the throne in 1175 under the name of Li Cao Ton and reigned until 1210. The two kings of Champa were, as I have just explained, the king of Vijaya and the king of Panduranga.

We know that the tribute of water symbolized allegiance and vassaldom. Even today at the courts of Phnom Penh and Bangkok, on the occasion of the coronation, the holy water for the anointing is gathered from the principal rivers of the various provinces of the kingdom.

The vassaldom which was very real for the two kings of Champa must have been considerably less effective for the distant king of Java and even less so for the emperor of Annam. But we know how readily oriental sovereigns accepted a nominal suzerainty which cost them little and assured them the good will of their neighbours.

In any case Jayavarman VII's prestige must have been great enough so that matrimonial alliance with his family was coveted. 'To those on whom he had already bestowed riches', says the stele at Prah Khan, 'he gave his seductively beautiful daughters in marriage.' In the meantime he had suffered a cruel loss. The queen had died, having spread good deeds around her and having collected for the principal sanctuaries of the kingdom a list of riches long enough to cover the whole length of a stele at the Royal Palace. She had, as we have seen, an older sister who according to the inscriptions, 'surpassed the wisdom of the philosophers in her knowledge', and whom the king had appointed head professor in a Buddhist monastery where she gave instruction to women. Jayavarman VII, after the death of his wife, married this older sister and gave her the title of first queen. But this high position did not deflect her from the pursuit of science. 'To women whose great desire was for science, she extended the favours of the king, like a delicious nectar, in the form of knowledge.' She was the author of the inscription from the Royal Palace from which I have quoted so often, worded in the purest Sanskrit.

The exact date of Jayavarman VII's death is not known. We know for a certainty that he was still reigning in 1201, the date at which he sent an emissary to the court of China. There is some evidence to lead us to think that he died about 1219 at a very advanced age.

Physically he was rather a plump man, with large features, who wore his hair pulled up to the top of his head forming a little chignon. His features are familiar to us from the bas-reliefs. In addition there are two statues and two heads, all with very similar features, which must be of the same man. I believe they are all images of Jayavarman VII. One of the statues was found at Angkor Thom and is now in the National Museum at Phnom Penh. The other, from P'imai near Korat, is now in the National Museum at Bangkok. Of the two heads, one is preserved in Marseille, and the other was only recently found at Prah Khan in Kompong Thom.

In connexion with the death of Jayavarman VII of which I have said we know neither the cause nor the cir-

---

21. Bas-relief on inner wall of Terrace of Leper King, twelfth century, originally intended to be hidden. This inner wall represented the subterranean slopes of Mount Meru, which was supposed to extend as far into the underworld as it rose in the sky.

Photograph by courtesy of USIS, Cambodia.

cumstances, we may wonder whether he was not afflicted
with the dread sickness which wasted his contemporary,
Baudouin IV of Jerusalem, the 'leper king'. Two bas-
reliefs of the time, one of which forms the pediment of
the chapel known as the hospital, east of the temple of
Takeo, represent according to the experts, treatment of
a secondary symptom of leprosy known medically as
'claw-hand' which is characterized by permanent con-
traction of the fingers. Goloubew has studied these bas-
reliefs in connexion with his research on the legend of
a leper king of Angkor, who I hasten to say had no connexion with the statue called by that name today. He
has been kind enough to send me the description of a
similar more detailed bas-relief from the Bayon, given him
in 1934 by Dr. Mesnard, Director of the Pasteur Institute:

> The forearms and hands of the patient are being care-
> fully examined by the women surrounding him. The
> action of one of them seems to me characteristic. She is
> holding the right little finger as if to straighten out the
> 'claw-hand'. Her gesture seems to be calling the attention
> of the others to this symptom.
>
> The patient's legs are resting on an object placed under
> his knees. One of the women is holding his right foot in
> her hand and is rubbing his right leg.
>
> The gestures of the woman seem to indicate that the
> extremities are affected with the painful nutritional defi-
> ciency typical of leprosy.
>
> Another important thing to notice is that on either side
> of the sick man there is a personage carrying a vase filled
> with round fruits. Might these not be the seeds of *krabao*?
> Hydnocarpus anthelmintica, called *krabao*, is a tree found

---

22. The so-called 'Leper King' was probably a god of death, who once
held a staff in his right hand. This popular appellation is due solely to his
lichen-covered body which gives the appearance of leprosy. Jayavarman
VII may have suffered from leprosy, but this statue is not a representation
of him.

all through the forests of Angkor. The Cambodians, even today, treat lepers by giving them the roasted seeds of *krabao* to eat.

This may possibly be a leper with the secondary symptoms of leprosy.

The sick man pictured on the pediment of the chapel at Takeo, as well as the one on the bas-relief of the Bayon, is certainly a personage of high rank, possibly the king himself. One is tempted to connect these pictures with the legend of a leprous king, which persists in Cambodia, and which may therefore have had some basis in fact. There is an echo of this myth in a medieval Hindu text which tells of the pilgrimage to India of a Cambodian king afflicted with leprosy. Possibly Jayavarman VII's founding of one hundred and two hospitals had some connexion with this sickness. If the king had leprosy he may have hoped that by founding these hospitals to care for his subjects, some credit might accrue to himself which would relieve his suffering. Or if he was healthy himself, he may have undertaken this medical philanthropy so that the benefits would reflect on one of his relatives sick with this affliction, which was generally considered a punishment for former sins.

From these few biographical facts emerges the figure of an energetic and ambitious man, who after long years of waiting and trials saved his country from conquest and lifted it to the peak of its power. The inscriptions describe him as a fervent Buddhist, honouring, says the stele at Ta Prohm, 'the high path which leads to supreme enlightenment, the unique doctrine without obstacle to attain a comprehension of reality, the law which the immortal honour in the three worlds, the sword which destroys the jungle of the passions'. He took over this faith from his father who had broken with the tradition of his Hindu predecessors, and according to the same stele, 'found his satisfaction in the nectar which is the religion of Sakyamuni', Buddhism of the Greater Vehicle, centred in the worship of Lokesvara.

The personality of Jayavarman VII which appears only dimly from the inscriptions I have quoted, found its full expression in the architectural work he left behind him, but which before Stern's research of 1927, was incorrectly thought to belong two centuries earlier, at the end of the ninth century.

This architectural work included Angkor Thom with its walls twelve kilometres on a side, its large moats and its five gates with the Bayon at the centre. It included Banteay Kdei, Ta Prohm, Prah Khan, Neak Pean, Ta Som, Krol Ko, Ta Nei. It included the enormous Banteay Chmar in the northwest, Vat Nokor at Kompong Cham, Ta Prohm at Bati. It included the one hundred and twenty-one rest houses for the use of pilgrims, strung out along the banked-up roads, many of which were also laid out by him. It included the one hundred and two hospitals spread out over the four corners of the kingdom. No other Cambodian king can claim to have moved so much stone.

We will review the more important of these monuments, whose original names, when we know them, always begin with the prefix Jaya, 'victory', which marked them as if with a seal with the name of the builder.

Perhaps the earliest is Banteay Kdei, east of the capital, on a former site, and flanked on the east by the magnificent basin, full of water at every season, called Sras Srang, or Royal Bath. The foundation stele of Banteay Kdei has not been found. Its original name and its purpose are unfortunately not known.

Ta Prohm is so close to Banteay Kdei that the south-east corner of its enclosure almost touches the north-west corner of Banteay Kdei. It was dedicated in 1186 to shelter the image of the queen mother in the likeness of Prajnaparamita, 'the Perfection of Wisdom', as well as two hundred and sixty other images including the master, or spiritual father of the king.

The great stele is still in place and gives us abundant details about the number of personnel in the temple, its property, and all the supplies needed for the cult. The stele says that the temple owned 3,140 villages and that its service required 79,365 people, of whom 18 were great priests, 2,740 officiates, 2,202 assistants, and 615 dancers. The property included a set of golden dishes weighing more than 500 kilograms, and almost as big a service in silver, 35 diamonds, 40,620 pearls, 4,540 precious stones, an enormous golden bowl, 876 veils from China, 512 silk beds, 523 parasols. Then comes a list of supplies of all kinds needed for the daily offerings, rice, butter, milk, molasses, oil, seeds, and also the amount needed for special feasts, and a list of goods furnished each year by the royal treasury, seeds, milk, honey, oil, wax, sandal, camphor, 2,387 sets of clothing to adorn the statues.

The inscription ends, ' Doing these good deeds, the king with extreme devotion to his mother, made this prayer: that because of the virtue of the good deeds I have accomplished, my mother, once delivered from the ocean of transmigration, may enjoy the state of Buddha.'

In 1191, five years after the building of Ta Prohm, the king inaugurated the temple known today as Prah

Khan, north of the capital, which was intended to shelter the statue of his father, Dharanindravarman II, in the likeness of Bodhisattva Lokesvara.

Inside the temple of Prah Khan, the central image was surrounded by a whole pantheon, about which we know from the little inscriptions at the entrances to the chapels. A stele found in 1939 tells us there were 430 images. As at Ta Prohm the Sanskrit inscription gives us the list of necessary furnishings for the sacred service and for the maintenance of the personnel. They are the same provisions but even more plentiful, furnished either from the royal stores, or by the 5,324 villages, totalling 97,840 taxpayers of both sexes.

The stele enumerates the monuments attached to Prah Khan, including among others the temples of Krol Ko and Ta Som, and the little sanctuary of Neak Pean, 'an eminent island, whose charm lies in its surrounding ponds which cleanse the soil of sins from those who visit it'.

While Ta Prohm was the mausoleum of the queen mother, Prah Khan was the funerary temple of King Dharanindravarman II, father of Jayavarman VII. The similar purpose for which these two monuments were built gives rise to some speculation.

We know the popularity of the Buddhist trinity, the Buddha, Bodhisattva Lokesvara, and Prajnaparamita. These three are invoked at the start of every one of Jayavarman VII's inscriptions. They are found together innumerable times in the sculpture, either in stone, bronze, or on the small votive tablets. If Ta Prohm sheltered the image of the king's mother as Prajnaparamita, and Prah Khan contained the image of his father in the guise of Lokesvara, where was the image of Buddha which was normally placed between the two?

Very probably this third image was in the Bayon, the central temple of the city of Angkor Thom, where the giant statue of Buddha was found which represented the 'Buddha-king', the Buddhist substitute for the former *linga* Devaraja, or god-king of the earlier reigns. Thus they created on a kilometric scale, appropriate to a great king, this triad which heretofore had only been produced in small sculpture.

The Bayon is located in the geometric centre of the city constructed by Jayavarman VII in the last years of his reign, a new city which probably encircled some earlier monuments in its enclosure, but which had the one essential feature, an entirely new temple and walls. Four axial avenues led out from the Bayon, as well as a fifth leading from the eastern entrance of the Royal Palace, a heritage of earlier reigns. They ended in five monumental gates which reproduced the characteristic motif of the temple, that is the towers sculptured with giant faces. The massive walls were twelve kilometres on a side and were surrounded by big moats. Outside the walls an ingenious system of irrigation spread fertility to the environs of the capital. I have described in a previous chapter how the Bayon was a kind of pantheon where both the family cults of the king and the provincial cults of the whole kingdom were housed. In the same way that the city with its central mountain and its enclosure constituted a small replica of the universe, the Bayon was a reduced image of the kingdom.

We can hardly doubt that Jayavarman VII looked on himself as a living Buddha when we see that he consecrated the temple of Ta Prohm to his mother, represented in the sanctuary in the guise of the spiritual mother of Buddha.

But there is even more evidence. Among the many religious foundations of the king listed on the stele of Prah Khan, there are twenty-three statues called Jaya Buddhamahanatha, consecrated in as many cities, among which are Lopburi, Sup'an, Ratburi, P'echaburi and Muong Sing, all today in Thai territory. Perhaps it was to house statues of this type that some of the provincial sanctuaries were built, sanctuaries whose style indicates that they belonged to the time of Jayavarman VII, for example Vat Nokor at Kompong Cham and Ta Prohm at Bati. We know with certainty from an inscription that there was a statue of the same name at Banteay Chmar, in a big monument consecrated to one of the sons of Jayavarman VII, Prince Srindrakumara, and to four companions in arms who had saved his life. This was during his combat with the monster Rahu and again in the course of an expedition in Champa. In another instance the short inscriptions on the Bayon name two of the same statues mentioned on the stele at Prah Khan which were probably replicas of the images worshipped in two of the provincial sanctuaries.

I am inclined to believe that these provincial statues of Buddha, of which our museums have several examples, were portrait statues of Jayavarman VII, represented with the attributes of Buddha, similar to the ones at the Bayon. Their titles all begin with the prefix Jaya, 'victory', which was another name for Jayavarman himself, and which constituted a kind of distinguishing seal on all his works. The titles all continue with the word *mahanatha*, 'the great saviour', a term which could apply to no one better than to Jayavarman VII, since he had saved the kingdom ten years before, driving the Chams from the country and even carrying the war into their own territory.

The consecration of the statues at the beginning of the reign of Jayavarman VII perhaps marked a decisive point in the shift from the cult of the preceding reigns to Buddhism. Jayabuddha was the Buddhist version of the title given by the former kings to the *lingas* which they erected on their pyramids. Indresvara had been erected by Indravarman on the summit of Bakong. Yasodharesvara had been consecrated by Yasovarman on the summit of Bakheng. Rajendrabhadresvara was erected by Rajendravarman in the central sanctuary of Pre Rup. The consecration of the Jayabuddhamahanatha in twenty-three cities, most of which were on the outer edges of the kingdom, proclaimed both the political authority of the king and his religious dominance. The names of two of these statues were repeated at the Bayon. If we had all the inscriptions from the Bayon, it is extremely probable that we would find all the twenty-three names of the Jayabuddhamahanatha there.

The Bayon situated in the middle of the microcosm of the royal city represented the focus of all the local sanctuaries and centralized the 'double power, secular and divine' which each of the sanctuaries of the Jayabuddhamahanatha represented in the distant provinces. If it is true, as I surmise, that the construction of the central mass of the Bayon, not originally planned, was for the purpose of installing the Buddharaja at its centre, the great statue of Buddha found in 1933 which was the Buddhist substitute for the former Devaraja, we can then go on to suppose that this giant Buddha was the sum of all the local Jayabuddhas whose images appeared in the lower gallery.

23. Balaha, the sacred horse, swimming through the central pool of Neak Pean, twelfth century. He is carrying the souls who cling to him to salvation in the central sanctuary.

In addition to these religious buildings there are other structures of a more utilitarian kind.

The stele at Prah Khan mentions one hundred and twenty-one 'houses with fire'[41] constructed along the roads that fanned out over the kingdom, fifty-seven on the road from Angkor to the capital of Champa, seventeen on the road from Angkor to P'imai in the plateau of Korat, forty-four leading to some cities of which we still do not know the location, one at Phnom Chisor, two unidentified. These were rest houses of which a few have been found, and which were spaced from twelve to fifteen kilometres apart, a distance which could be covered in four or five hours on foot. We know eight of the seventeen which bordered the road from Angkor to P'imai. Beng Mealea, Ta Prohm, Prah Khan, Banteay Chmar, each has its own, constructed in the temple enclosure to the east of the temple entrance.

Jayavarman VII thus covered his kingdom with a network of roads, enhanced at regularly spaced intervals by rest houses for stopping, very similar to the *tram** of the Annamite countries.

This system was still in existence a century later, and filled the Chinese envoy, Chou Ta Kuen, with admiration. In his account of his voyage he wrote, 'Along the important roads there are resting places similar to our posting houses.'

The creation of these rest houses went hand in hand with a widespread campaign for sanitation, which was evidenced by the one hundred and two hospitals scat-

---

*   resting place at end of a day's travel

24. Jayavarman VII, National Museum, Phnom Penh, twelfth century. A number of similar statues have been found, and are also presumed to be his likenesses.

tered over the country and which were certainly made possible by the system of roads.[42]

These shelters for the sick were certainly built of light materials. The sick would not have been housed in stone or brick buildings, since such permanent buildings were reserved for gods only, and even the most important people, such as the kings themselves, lived in wooden houses. Thus, the only hope of locating a hospital would be by finding its foundations, which might indicate the plan and arrangement of the rooms. But as we shall see, each hospital included a chapel which was built of stone, and which, with the inevitable enclosing wall, constituted the stone skeleton of these establishments.

We know for certain the sites of seventeen of them, thanks to the discovery of their foundation steles written in Sanskrit, each with an identical text. Nine of these sites have buildings recognizable as belonging to the style of Jayavarman VII's time. They have identical dimensions and are all built on the same plan and have common features. These are a tower in the centre opening to the east onto a porch or foyer, either in sandstone or laterite; south-east of the tower a small attached building opening to the west; an enclosing wall of laterite broken on the east by a *gopura,* or entrance pavilion, of cruciform shape and of the same material as the tower; and generally a pool outside the enclosure.

The similarity of their plan and style, as well as the identical steles, allow us to conclude that these are the stone remains of Jayavarman VII's hospitals.

Moreover this arrangement is repeated in seventeen additional monuments which seem to be of the same epoch. We can now say that we know the location of thirty-three of the hospitals of Jayavarman VII, that is, about a third. More will probably be found, but we can never hope to find them all because some of them were probably constructed entirely of perishable materials.

The foundation steles give us interesting information about their organization. After the Buddhist invocations and the traditional eulogy of the king, the inscription tells us that the hospital is placed under the auspices of Buddha the Healer, Bhaishajyaguru Vaiduryaprabha, 'the master of remedies, with the shining beryl', whose statue was placed in the chapel adjoining the hospital. He was one of the most popular Buddhas, and still is today in China and Tibet.

The four castes could be cared for in the establishment. There were two doctors, each assisted by a man and two women, two store-keepers with the job of giving out medicine, two cooks having the responsibility of the fuel and water as well as for cleaning the temple, two servitors to prepare the offerings for Buddha, fourteen hospital attendants, six women to heat the water and to grind the medicines, and two women to pound the rice. The total number of workers who were housed was thirty-two. Besides them there were sixty-six lodged at their own expense, making a total of ninety-eight. Rice for offerings to the divinities was fixed at a bushel a day, and the leftovers were given to the patients. The list of provisions taken three times a year in the royal stores included honey, sugar, camphor, sesame, spices, black mustard, cumin, nutmeg, coriander, fennel, cardoman, ginger, cubeb, vetiver, cinnamon, myrobalan, jujube vinegar, the quantities of each of which are exactly stated.

Besides the provincial hospitals whose management we have just described there were also a certain number of more important establishments in the big centres, es-

pecially at Angkor. The foundations of four of them
have been found near the four gates of the city of Angkor
Thom. This explains why on the stele at Ta Prohm the
figures for the total amount of provisions are far greater
than the annual expenditures for all of the hospitals
together. Thus what might be called government health
service consumed 11,192 tons of rice annually, produced
by 838 villages with a population of 81,640 people. The
hospitals used 2,124 kilograms of sesame, 105 kilograms
of cardoman and 3,402 nutmegs, 48,000 febrifuges, 1,960
boxes of salve for hemorrhoids, and so on in propor-
tionate amounts.

One fact that is noticeable immediately is that the
institutions were not concerned only with medical and
social problems. Morality and religion seem also to have
been in the mind of the founder. 'He felt the afflictions
of his subjects more than his own', declares the edict,
'because the suffering of the people constitute the suffering of the king, more than his own suffering.' The
concept is clearly stated that the king is responsible for
the prosperity of the state, maintaining a proper order
by his punctual performance of the necessary rites, ca-
pable of causing calamity by bad conduct, and acutely
aware of the burdens of his subjects.

Since in the Buddhist belief, sickness was supposed to
be the deserved retribution for errors committed in previous existences, moral purification was at least as important as medical treatment. From the king's point of
view the beneficent influence of the Buddhist gods, under
whose auspices the hospitals functioned, was worth as
much as the medical care or the medicines administered.

By spreading the benefits of medical assistance among
his people, from the Buddhist standpoint Jayavarman

VII was accomplishing a meritorious work. 'Full of deep sympathy for the good of the world', the edict on the hospitals continues, 'the king expresses this wish: all the souls who are plunged in the ocean of existence, may I be able to rescue them by virtue of this good work. May all the kings of Cambodia, devoted to the right, carry on my foundation, and attain for themselves and their descendants, their wives, their officials, their friends, a holiday of deliverance in which there will never be any sickness.'

I have tried to give an idea of the amplitude of Jayavarman VII's constructions by enumerating these principal foundations. His vast programme of medical assistance has sufficed, as I said earlier, to make us revise our evaluation of him, beginning with the discovery of the first hospital stele.

But every medal has its reverse side. We must consider what these undertakings meant to the Cambodian people who, by the sweat of their brows just fifty years before, had built Angkor Wat, Banteay Samre, Beng Mealea, a large part of Prah Vihear. We must think what the construction of religious buildings like the Bayon cost. One must visualize the armies of carriers, slaving on the slopes of Phnom Kulen, of porters dragging these enormous blocks of sandstone, of the masons fitting the stones together, of the sculptors and decorators, these human ants, not inspired by the collective faith of the builders of our cathedrals, but recruited by conscription to erect mausoleums for the glory of their princes, into which they would never be allowed to enter. And there were not only the labourers on the construction; in 1191 after only ten years of the reign, when the programme was not yet completed, there were according to the stele at Prah Khan more than 20,000 images in gold, silver, bronze and stone spread all over the kingdom. The service of their cult required 306,372 servitors, living in 13,500 villages, and consuming 38,000 tons of rice yearly. And what riches were accumulated in these temples! Thousands of kilograms of gold and silver, tens of thousands of gems and pearls, without counting the enormous quantities of supplies of all sorts requisitioned for their sacred service.

We cannot verify whether such quantities of riches really existed, but what we can see with our own eyes is the accumulation of the stones shaped by the will of the king, the feverish haste with which they were put in place without even waiting for the builders to fit the joints properly, the worn-out sandstone replaced by laterite, the uncompleted bas-reliefs, the mediocrity of the careless decoration. Jayavarman, who was no longer young, wanted at all costs to accomplish a programme that was vast enough to last for several reigns. What exactly happened after his death? We know from inscriptions that his immediate successors repudiated Buddhism of the Greater Vehicle to revert to Hindu traditions. We can see that the monuments show the traces of this change. We can be certain that he died leaving the country worn out by his megalomania and thenceforth unable to resist the attacks of his young and turbulent neighbour to the west. In 1296 when the Chinese envoy, Chou Ta Kuen, came to Cambodia, he found the country devastated 'following a war with the Siamese during which', he said, 'the entire population had been forced to fight.'

Louis Finot said in an excellent lecture in 1908:

> There is no evidence that these people resisted the aggression with vigour. They perhaps even looked on it as a deliverance. If one considers that they had been forced not only

to supply the labour for contructing these gigantic monuments, whose size is astonishing even today, but also to provide the service and the supplies for the maintenance of the innumerable sanctuaries scattered over the whole empire, which as has been said of France of the eleventh century was clothed in a garment of temples, we cannot be surprised that after several centuries of this regime, the hardworking population was decimated and spent. Surely they did not defend these rapacious gods or these slave-drivers and collectors of tithes with much ardour. The conqueror on the other hand offered the vanquished a precious compensation ; he offered them a gentle religion whose doctrine of resignation suited this tired and discouraged people most appealingly. This religion was economical, its ministers were pledged to poverty, contenting themselves with a straw roof and a handful of rice, a moral religion whose principles assured peace of soul and social tranquility. We can understand why the Khmer people accepted it without repugnance and happily put aside the burden of their former glory.

This religion so aptly described by Louis Finot who knew it well, was Buddhism of the Lesser Vehicle, imported from Ceylon to Siam through the Mons and the Burmans. Basically opposed to individual personality, this Buddhism without deities, so different from that of Jayavarman VII, could not but destroy the cult which was both personal and nationalistic, and which forced the people to worship the god-king and the deified princes. Very probably this new faith played an important part in the rapid decadence of the Khmer Empire in the fourteenth century.

And today there is nothing left of the splendour of Angkor but ruins guarded by the haunting smile of Jayavarman VII, their great ruler who looked upon himself as the living Buddha.

Glossary

Amithaba	Buddha of the highest order, pictured on the turban of Bodhisattva
angkor	town
apsara	celestial dancer
banteay	citadel
baray	reservoir
beng	pond
Bodhisattva	one who is in the process of becoming Buddha
Brahma	the creator, one of the gods of the Brahman trinity, usually represented with four faces, and often mounted on *hamsa*
Buddha	divine man who attained supreme enlightenment
Cham	inhabitant of Champa
Champa	rival empire of the Khmers, of Hindu culture, on the coast of Annam
deva	god
devata	goddess
dharma	law, religion, royal authority or cult
dvarapala	temple guardian
Ganesa	son of Siva, with human body and elephant head
Ganga	the goddess of the Ganges, one of the consorts of Siva
garuda	divine bird, with predatory beak and claws, and human body
gopura	entrance pavilion, or stone platform in front of a temple

hamsa	sacred goose, Brahma's mount
Harihara	a god, half Hari (Vishnu), half Hara (Siva)
Hinayana	Lesser Vehicle of Buddhism
Indra	Brahman god, wielder of thunderbolts, usually mounted on a three-headed elephant
Isvara	one of the names of Siva
jaya	victory
Kailasa	Himalayan peak, home of Siva
Kambu	mythical hero who was the ancestor of the Kambujas, today the Cambodians
Kambuja	Cambodia
kamrateng anh	my lord
kamrateng jagat	lord of the universe
ko	bull
kompong	village, or wharf
Krishna	incarnation of Vishnu
kumbhanda	class of mythical demons
Laksmi	consort of Vishnu, goddess of beauty, riches and happiness
linga	phallic symbol, one of the forms of Siva
Lokesvara	the Compassionate Bodhisattva, wearing a turban decorated with Amithaba, and with four arms, carrying the lotus, the rosary, the flask, and the book.
Mahabharata	famous Hindu epic
mahanatha	great saviour
Mahayana	Greater Vehicle of Buddhism
Maitreya	future Buddha
makara	composite sea monster with an elephant head, often pictured spewing forth a *naga*
men	pavilion for burning the dead

Meru	sacred mountain at the centre of the world, home of the gods
mudra	symbolic gesture of the hands of Buddha, indicating his 'attitude'
mukhalinga	*linga* decorated with a head in bas-relief
naga	cobra in stylized form with multiple heads
Nagaraja	king of the *nagas*
nandin	sacred bull, mount of Siva
Parvati	consort of Siva
phnom	mountain
prah	sacred
Prajnaparamita	perfection of wisdom, mother of Buddha
prasat	sanctuary tower
prei	forest
Rahu	monster who swallows the sun during an eclipse
raja	ruler
raksha	guardian demon
Rama	incarnation of Vishnu, hero of Ramayana
Ramayana	Hindu epic, the story of Rama and Siva
Ravana	Demon king of the Rakshas with multiple heads and arms
rishi	Brahman ascetic
Sakyamuni	one of the names of Buddha
sanjak	royal servitor sworn to loyalty by an oath taken in blood
Sita	wife of Rama
Siva	the Creator and Destroyer, one of the three gods of the Brahman trinity, usually represented with a third eye in his forehead. The sacred *linga* was worshipped as symbol of Siva

srah	pond
srei	woman
Sri	consort of Vishnu
stupa	funerary temple
Surgriva	king of the monkeys, dethroned by his brother Valin
Surya	sun god
ta	ancestor
tevoda	female divinity
thom	large
Uma	consort of Siva
ushnisha	protuberance on top of Buddha's head
Valin	brother and usurper of Surgriva, king of monkeys
varman	the protected, protégé
Veda	sacred book of Brahmans
vihara	monastery
Vishnu	the Protector, one of the gods of the Brahman trinity, generally with four arms holding the disc, the conch shell, the ball and the club
Visvakarman	divine architect, brother of Siva
wat	pagoda
yaksha	good or evil spirit
Yama	God of Death, mounted on a buffalo

References

Page

[1]P. Pelliot : 'Le Fou-nan', *Bulletin de l'Ecole Française d'Extrême-Orient*, 1903.   1

[2]G. Cœdès : 'La tradition généalogique des premiers rois d'Angkor', *Bulletin de l'Ecole Française d'Extrême-Orient*, 1928.   2 & 4

[3]G. Cœdès : 'A propos du Tchen-la d'eau', *Bulletin de l'Ecole Française d'Extrême-Orient*, 1936.   2

[4]G. Cœdès : 'Les capitales de Jayavarman II', *Bulletin de l'Ecole Française d'Extrême-Orient*, 1928.   3 & 74
[5]G. Cœdès : 'Deux inscriptions sanskrites du Founan', *Bulletin de l'Ecole Française d'Extrême-Orient*, 1931.   4

[6]H. Parmentier : 'L'art présumé du Fou-nan', *Bulletin de l'Ecole Française d'Extrême-Orient*, 1932.   5

[7]H. Parmentier : 'Publications de l'Ecole Française', XXI–XXII, 1927.   5

[8]For the successive theories on the chronology of the Khmer monuments see :
P. Stern : 'Le Bayon d'Angkor Thom et l'évolution de l'art khmèr', *Ann. du Musée Guimet, Bibl. de vulgarisation*, 47 ;
G. Cœdès : 'La date du temple de Bantéay Srei', *Bulletin de l'Ecole Française d'Extrême-Orient*, 1929 ;
V. Goloubev : 'Le Phnom Bakheng et la ville de Yaçovarman', *Bulletin de l'Ecole Française d'Extrême-Orient*, 1933.   6

[9]For an account of the early Cambodian studies, see G. Cœdès's descriptive bibliography of works on the archaeology of Cambodia and Champa in the *Bulletin de la Commission archéologique de l'Indochine*, 1909.   10

[10]The account of the voyage of Chou Ta-kuen was translated in 1902 by P. Pelliot in the *Bulletin de l'Ecole Française d'Extrême-Orient*.   15

Page

[11]For a full discussion of portraiture in Khmer sculpture see G. Cœdès: 'Le Portrait dans l'Art Khmèr', *Arts Asiatiques*, Tome VII, fasicule 3, 1960.   22

[12]For the translations of the inscriptions on the Bayon, see *Bulletin de l'Ecole Française d'Extrême-Orient*, 1928.   24

[13]A. Foucher : *Bulletin de la Commission Archéologique de l'Indochine*, 1910, p. 135.   27

[14]For more detail, see G. Cœdès: 'La destination funéraire des grands monuments khmèrs', *Bulletin de l'Ecole Française d'Extrême-Orient*, 1940.   27

[15]W. F. Stutterheim : *Indian Influences in Old Balinése Art*, London, 1935.   28

[16]P. Stern's articles on the temple-mountain in *Bulletin de l'Ecole Française d'Extrême-Orient*, 1934, and in the *Bulletin de la Société des Etudes Indochinoises*, 1937.   30

[17]J. Przyluski : 'Pradakshina et prasavya en Indochine', *Festshrift für M. Winternitz zum 70ten Geburtstag*, 1933, p. 320.   34

[18]R. von Heine-Geldern : 'Weltbild und Bauform in Südostasien', *Wiener Beiträge zur Kunst und Kultur Asiens*, 1930.   39

[19]The hypothesis of Dr. F. D. K. Bosch, former head of the Service archéologique des Indes Néerlandaises.   45

[20]P. Mus : 'Angkor in the Time of Jayavarman VII', *Indian Art and Letters*, 1937.   46

[21]De Coral-Rémusat : 'Animaux fantastiques de l'Indochine, de l'Insulinde et de la Chine', *Bulletin de l'Ecole Française d'Extrême-Orient*, 1936.   48

[22]G. Cœdès : 'Quelques suggestions sur la méthode à suivre pour interpréter les bas-reliefs de Bantéay Chmar et de la galerie extérieure du Bayon', *Bulletin de l'Ecole Française d'Extrême-Orient*, 1932.   50

[23]Doudart de Lagrée et Francis Garnier : *Voyage d'exploration en Indochine effectué pendant les années 1866, 1867, et 1868 par une Commission Française*, 2 vols, Paris, Hachette et Cie., n.d.   54

                                                    Page
24LOUIS DELAPORTE :   *Voyage en Cambodge—L'Architecture
Khmère*, Paris, Delagrave, 1880.   54 & 61

25A. TISSANDIER :   *Cambodge et Java 1893–1894*, Paris,
Masson, 1896.   54

26LUCIEN FOURNEREAU ET JACQUES PORCHER :   *Les Ruines
d'Angkor*, Paris, Ernest Leroux, 1890.   54

27H. PARMENTIER :   'Modifications subies par le Bayon
au cours de son exécution', *Bulletin de l'Ecole Française
d'Extrême-Orient*, 1927.   58

28J. MOURA :   *Le royaume du Cambodge*, 1883. II, Paris,
E. Leroux, 1883, pp. 21–22.   60

29J. HARMAND :   *Notes de voyage en Indochine, Annales de
l'Extrême-Orient*, I, 1878–1879.   61

30JEAN COMMAILLE :   *Guide aux Ruines d'Angkor*, Paris,
Librairie Hachette, 1912.   61

31HENRI DUFOUR ET CHARLES CARPEAUX :   *Le Bayon
d'Angkor Thom Bas-reliefs publiés par les soins de la Commission Archéologique de l'Indochine par la Mission Henri
Dufour avec la Collaboration de Charles Carpeaux*, Paris,
Ernest Leroux, 1910.   61

32P. STERN :   'Travaux exécutés au Phnom Kulên', *Bulletin de l'Ecole Française d'Extrême-Orient*, 1938.   68

33P. DUPONT :   'Les monuments du Phnom Kulên, I. Le
Prasat Néak Ta', *Bulletin de l'Ecole Française d'Extrême-
Orient*, 1938.   68

34G. CŒDÈS :   'Le royaume de Çrîvijaya', *Bulletin de
l'Ecole Française d'Extrême-Orient*, 1918.   70

35G. FERRAND :   *Relations de voyages et textes géographiques
arabes, persans, et turcks, relatifs à l'Extrême-Orient*, Paris,
1913.   71

36H. MARCHAL :   'Kutiçvara', *Bulletin de l'Ecole Française
d'Extrême-Orient*, 1937.   75

37P. STERN :   'Hariharâlaya et Indrapura', *Bulletin de
l'Ecole Francaise d'Extrême-Orient*, 1938.   76

Page

[38]P. STERN : 'Le style de Kulên', *Bulletin de l'Ecole Française d'Extrême-Orient*, 1938.　　79

[39]P. STERN : Etudes d'orientalisme publiées par le Musée Guimet à la mémoire de Raymonde Linossier, t. II　　80

[40]MA TUAN LIN : *Ethnographie des peuples etrangères à la chinois* (traduit par le Marquis d'Hervey de Saint Denys), Paris, Ernest Leroux, 1883.　　89

[41]G. CŒDÈS : 'Les gîtes d'étape à la fin du XIIe siècle', *Bulletin de l'Ecole Française d'Extrême-Orient*, 1940.　　101

[42]G. CŒDÈS : 'L'assistance médicale au Cambodge à la fin du XIIe siècle', *Revue médicale française d'Extrême-Orient*, 1941.　　102

Available Tourist Guides to Angkor

In English

1. *Angkor, Guide Henri Parmentier*
   Albert Portail, Editeur, Saigon
   Printed in Phnom Penh, Cambodia, 1959

   148 pp. paper-bound booklet with illustrations and 2 maps, translated from the French

2. *A Preface to Angkor*
   Prepared with the assistance of the Ecole Française d'Extrême-Orient by the National Tourist Office of Cambodia, Phnom Penh, 1960

   38 pp. paper-bound booklet with brief descriptions, chronology, and tourist advice

In French

1. *Les Monuments du Groupe d'Angkor, Guide*
   by Maurice Glaize
   Albert Portail, Editeur, Saigon, 1948

   280 pp. with detailed history and description of each monument, arranged geographically, with index, charts, maps, illustrations, including both Angkor and Roluos

2. French edition of *Guide Parmentier* described above